The Magic Lamp

How To Make Certain Your Wishes Come True

KEITH ELLIS

THREE WATERS PRESS
BOSTON, VIRGINIA

The Magic Lamp

How To Make Certain Your Wishes Come True

KEITH ELLIS

Published by:

THREE WATERS PRESS
349 Turkey Ridge Road, Suite 100
Boston, Virginia, 22713
Phone: 540-547-3537
Fax: 540-547-4245
Email: lamp@selfhelp.com

Printed on recycled paper in the United States of America.

Library of Congress Catalog Card Number 95-060104
ISBN 0-9645453-0-6

Warning—Disclaimer

This book is designed to provide information in regard to the subject matter covered. It is sold with the understanding that the publisher and author are not engaged in rendering legal, accounting, counselling, or other professional services or advice. If you require legal or other expert assistance, you should seek the services of a competent professional.

The purpose of this book is to educate and entertain. The author and Three Waters Press shall have neither liabilty nor responsiblity to any person or entity with respect to any loss or damage caused, or alleged to have been caused, directly or indirectly by the information or ideas contained or suggested in this book.

If you do not wish to be bound by the above, you may return this book to the publisher for a refund.

To Mom,
who taught me how
to believe in myself.

Acknowledgments

Unlike someone making a speech at the Oscars, I don't have to pretend that I haven't thought at great length about what I want to say. I have. I owe more than I can express to more good people than I can count. But a few of these people have had such a marked influence on me, and on this book, that I want to thank them by name.

Thanks to Margaret Ellis, my wife, who gave me love, understanding, and support when I disappeared for hours every day to work on *The Magic Lamp*. Thanks also for her invaluable help in editing the finished product.

Thanks to Barbara Ellis, my mother, who besides being a great mother and a wonderful human being, is also a fine writer who helped to edit this book.

Thanks to Alan Ellis, my brother, who is the finest wordsmith I know, and one of the most inspirational thinkers. Time after time he came up with great ideas for what I should say in *The Magic Lamp*, and how I should say it, then let me claim the credit for his thoughts as if they were my own.

Finally, thanks to all the writers and thinkers, the speakers and doers I have studied for all these years. Many of them are listed in the "Resources" section at the back of this book. Many more are not. To all of them I offer my humble gratitude. When you stand on the shoulders of giants, it's easier to glimpse the sky.

On the Use of Personal Pronouns

In the English language the indefinite personal pronouns *he*, *him*, and *his* refer to indefinite persons of both sexes. Many women take exception to this. Most men would too, if it worked the other way around.

There are two ways to fix the problem: we can change the language, or we can change ourselves. I prefer the latter. Only then will the language follow.

Let us rid these pronouns of their political significance and thereby deny them the power to divide us. Let men writers use masculine pronouns, and we shall understand nothing more of this than that these writers are men. Let women writers use feminine pronouns, and we shall understand nothing more of this than that these writers are women. Then let readers see past the pronoun to the person. When the gender of a pronoun signifies nothing more than the gender of a writer—instead of the gender of reality—we will all be on the right path.

Contents

Section 4: Persist

Introduction

In 1953 Yale University surveyed its graduating class and discovered that only 3% had written goals. Twenty years later, Yale surveyed this same class and learned that the 3% who had written goals had amassed a net worth greater than that of the other 97% *combined*.

The moral of this story is:

1. Goals work.
2. Almost nobody uses them.

I'm living proof. For years I read every goal-setting book I could find. I listened to every goal-setting cassette I could beg, borrow, or buy. I attended every goal-setting seminar that came to town, and traveled to many that never made it to town. You'd better believe I knew that goals worked. I just never set any.

For one thing, they bored me. For another, they threatened me. They locked me in a cage when all I wanted was the freedom to be open to every opportunity, but the obligation to pursue none. I knew that goals worked, but I was never willing to put them to work.

Then in the shower one morning I remember daydreaming about the fame and fortune that would come my way if only I could make my wishes come true—like in a fairy tale. What a wonderful fantasy! Too bad there was a catch. In a fairy tale you could always count on a Fairy Godmother for help, or a Wizard, or a Genie. Unfortunately, all I could count on was myself.

That got my attention. What if I really could count on myself? What if I really could figure out exactly what I wanted from life and then make it happen, just like setting a goal?

BINGO! I finally struck brain!

Wishes *are* goals—but goals with snap, crackle, and pop. Goals provide the process that can take you where you want to go, but too often they don't provide the inspiration to get you there. Wishes are different. They have impact—like being struck by lightning instead of by a lightning bug. They let you dream. They let you soar. They let you tap into a source of limitless possibility and boundless energy that gives you the power to accomplish what you might otherwise never have imagined. If you want to make things happen in your life, don't think about goals—think about making your wishes come true.

I was so excited I nearly slipped on a bar of soap. Wishing was the answer I'd been seeking for years. I never felt much joy in rolling out of bed in the morning and telling myself, *Today I'm going to work on my goals.* But the thought of saying, *Today I'm going to make my wishes come true*, that made me feel like I could accomplish anything. It was like a missing spark that could set my life ablaze with success, prosperity, and happiness.

I stepped out of the shower, grabbed a notepad and began to write as fast as I could, trying to capture all the ideas that began pouring out of me faster than my hand could drag a pen across the paper. In the weeks that followed I transformed everything I knew about goal setting into a strategy for wishing. I named this strategy the LAMP Process. As soon as I committed my ideas to paper, I put them to work. As soon as I put them to work, I began to make my wishes come true.

The LAMP Process allowed me to go from minoring in achievement to majoring in success. I can't say it happened overnight—it didn't take that long. The moment I changed me, the world changed around me. The things I wanted to happen, began to happen. The kind of life I had been afraid even to dream about began to unfold before my eyes, like magic.

I've written *The Magic Lamp* to share with you this remarkable power to make your wishes come true. My intent is to offer a strategy, not a sermon. I'm not going to preach about motivation or try to sell you on success. I assume that you already want more from life than what you have and you're searching for a way to get it. That's exactly what you'll find here: a way to get it, whatever your background, whatever your age, whatever your circumstances.

But what about luck? Isn't it true that fortune—good or ill—is what ultimately determines our fate?

Luck performs its part in what happens to you; what you'll learn here is how to perform yours. Fortune deals the cards; what you'll learn here is how to play them. Fate rules but favors those who learn the rules. This book is about the most important rule of all—*cause and effect*.

Cause and Effect

Have you ever run a stop light and not been given a ticket? You were lucky; you got away with it. Have you ever jumped from a ten-story building and not been hurt? Don't try it. You won't get away with it. You might break the laws of man, but you can't break the laws of nature. If you try, they will only break you.

Consider the Law of Cause and Effect. No effect occurs without a cause; the cause must always precede the effect. Simple, inescapable, it's the easiest natural law to understand, and the easiest to forget.

Who would stand in front of a wood stove and demand heat without first filling the stove with wood? No one in his right mind. But how often have you heard someone swear that from now on he will do only what he is paid to do—and nothing more—unless he gets a raise? The Law of Cause and Effect says he'll have a long wait. He must first do more than he is being paid for, to make himself worth more than he is being paid.

Who would expect to make a withdrawal from a savings account before first making a deposit? No one in his right mind. But have you ever had a friend who demanded more from a relationship without first being willing to invest more in that relationship? Because of the Law of Cause and Effect, this kind of person will always be in for a big disappointment.

Who would stand before a patch of barren earth and demand vegetables without first planting a garden? No one in his right mind. But have you ever met someone who feels entitled to the rewards of success without first being willing to invest the time and effort it takes to become successful? According to the Law of Cause and Effect, the investment must always come first, if the rewards are to follow.

Life teaches us that we have to put wood in a wood stove *before* we get heat; we have to make a deposit *before* we can make a withdrawal; we have to plant seeds, water them, weed them, and nurture them *before* we can harvest our first ear of corn or pick our first tomato. Too often, we don't apply this knowledge to the way we run our lives.

When you desire a specific effect in your life—like a more meaningful relationship, a better job, or an important accomplishment—you must *first* set in motion the cause of that effect. If the cause is missing, the effect will be missing as well. If the effect is missing, you can be certain that you have neglected to set in motion the appropriate cause.

You can be equally certain that once you set in motion that cause, the effect you desire will follow—without fail—as reliably as the sun chases the first glimmer of dawn over the horizon. The cause must always come first. Once it does, you can count on the effect.

The most important decision you will ever make in life is this: *Do you choose to be a cause or an effect?* When you choose to be a cause, you make things happen. When you choose to be an effect, you settle for whatever happens to you.

When you choose to be a cause, you become the star quarterback of your own life, the Most Valuable Player of your own Super Bowl. When you choose to be an effect, you just watch from the stands. You're content to laugh and to cry, to live and to die, based on the actions of others.

The difference between being a cause and being an effect is the difference between being a hammer and being a nail. One acts; the other is acted upon. *The Magic Lamp* presents a strategy for those who would rather be a hammer than a nail.

The LAMP Process

The Magic Lamp shows you how to set in motion the causes that will produce the effects you want. I call this the LAMP Process. The letters *L*, *A*, *M*, and *P* each stand for one of the four major steps in the process. You can memorize these steps in less than a minute and apply them for the rest of your life. When you're done with this book, you will understand why you don't need iron-willed self-discipline to be successful. You will understand why you don't need to be particularly talented or intelligent to make your wishes come true. You just need to follow these four steps:

Step 1:   **L**ock On

Decide what you want to wish for. Think of it as choosing the effect you wish to cause. Once you have chosen that effect, lock onto it the way a guided missile locks onto its target.

Step 2:   **A**ct

Set in motion the causes that will make your wish come true.

Step 3:   **M**anage your progress

Track the causes you've set in motion to make sure that they are producing the effects you want. If they aren't, then adjust what you're doing.

Step 4:   *P*ersist

Finish what you start.

A crowbar is a tool that works according to the principle of *leverage*. The LAMP Process is a tool that works according to the principle of *cause and effect*. In both cases, the principle is what counts, not the tool. The principle is what makes things happen; the tool is merely the instrument. The next book you read may teach you a better tool than the LAMP Process, but you will never find a better principle than this one:

> *To get whatever you want from life you have only to set in motion the appropriate cause, and the effect will take care of itself.*

Fix this in your mind for now. It will open the entire world to you later.

LAMP Process

Step One:

Lock On

1

What Do You Want?

"I am master of earth and air and wave, but slave of the lamp and the bearer's slave. What will you have, Master, what will you have?"

The Genie of the Lamp,
from *One Thousand and
One Arabian Nights*

Imagine taking a stroll one balmy evening, when in the twilight you stumble across an ancient brass lamp, the kind you might find in a Turkish Bazaar. You stoop to retrieve the lamp and notice in the dimness an inscription carved along one side. Centuries of tarnish and neglect make the writing almost illegible, so you buff it two or three times with your sleeve. The lamp erupts in a blast of smoke and flame. Stumbling backward, you drop the lamp and shield your eyes. When you open them again, standing before you, as big as a billboard, is a Genie.

With a voice that rolls in like thunder from the horizon, he says, "I am the Genie of the Lamp. What will you have, Master, what will you have?" What would you ask the Genie to do?

Believe it or not, you hold in your hands an owner's manual for just such a lamp. Though it may look like an ordinary book, don't let that fool you. If you take to heart what you'll find in these pages, you'll unleash the power to grant yourself any wish you truly desire.

This power is locked in the human brain, that crinkled miracle that lurks just behind the eyes, the creator of everything from supercomputers to moon-landings to sliced bread. And you own such a brain, free and clear. Yours is the equal of any other brain on the planet. You are its sole proprietor, the only one who can summon its power, the master of a Genie that lies between your ears, brimming with the God-like power of creation. Congratulations!

But that still leaves you with the same problem, doesn't it? What will you ask the Genie to do?

Before you can make your wishes come true, you must first decide what to wish for. When people don't get what they want from life, usually it's because they don't know what they want. They grind through one work week after another, daydreaming about the good life, but they rarely muster a clear idea of what that "good life" should be. As competent and hardworking as they are, they lack purpose. They've been taught how to shoot, but they've never been taught how to aim.

Perhaps the most startling truth about human nature is that anyone can do something remarkable if he has something remarkable to do. Once you decide what you really want, the rest falls into place. You awaken each morning with a reason to get out of bed. Your days are filled with meaning because you fill them with meaningful work. You are able to take advantage of your talents, your time, and your opportunities because you have a purpose. Without this purpose the astonishing power you have to grant your own wishes sits idle, double-parked, the motor running with no one behind the wheel. But with this purpose, you shift smoothly through the gears, traveling at speeds beyond your comprehension.

Go ahead, slip into the driver's seat. Figure out what you really want. Not what you're supposed to want, not what someone else wants for you, but what you in your heart of hearts want for yourself.

Brainstorming

The easiest way to find out what you really want is to ask yourself. Specifically, ask your subconscious mind—the powerhouse of your intellect. The quality of the answers you receive will depend on how you ask your questions, so I suggest you use a tool that is designed specifically to help you tap the power of your subconscious mind. This tool is called *brainstorming*. I've outlined its five simple steps below.

Step 1:   *Write the topic you want to brainstorm, in the form of a question, at the top of a clean sheet of paper.*

The human mind is the most powerful computer on earth, but you don't have to learn a programming language to use it; all you have to do is to ask it a question.

Step 2:   Write whatever pops into your head.

Ask yourself the question you've written at the top of your page, then listen to your answers—all your answers. The best way to listen is to write your answers down. Write every thought that floats into your mind when you ask your question, even the silly thoughts, and the painful ones, and the ones that embarrass you, even the ones that seem to make no sense. Write them all, whether they seem useful or not, whether you approve of them or not. The first rule of brainstorming is to listen to yourself. If you don't, who will?

Step 3:   Accept with gratitude whatever pops into your head.

No matter how silly your thoughts may seem, no matter how impossible, or preposterous, or embarrassing, remind yourself how fortunate you are to have so many interesting ideas.

Think of each idea as a gift. We might not like every gift we receive, but we accept each one, we open each one, and we thank the giver. It's the thought that counts. If you accept all your thoughts gratefully, your subconscious—like any other giver of gifts—will be that much more willing to keep them coming.

Step 4:   Keep your pen moving.

Tell yourself you're going to write for a fixed amount of time—a minute, two minutes, five minutes—and then keep your pen moving until the time is up. Keep writing even if what you write seems like nonsense. Keep writing even if you have to write the same thing over and over. Keep writing, and sooner or later you will discover you have something to say.

Step 5:   Save your criticism for later.

Write, don't judge. You can judge later. Brainstorming is a tool to generate ideas, not to evaluate them.

Have you ever offered a suggestion in a meeting, only to have someone point out how stupid it was? After that, you probably learned to keep your thoughts to yourself.

Your subconscious is just as sensitive. If you reject its suggestions, it stops making them. It's like a faucet—either it's turned on or it's turned off. The purpose in brainstorming is to turn the faucet on full blast and keep it on. Generate as many ideas as you can. Let your writer flow, and let your editor go. You can sort it all out later.

There is no time like the present to begin your first official brainstorming session. So take out a blank sheet of paper and write this question at the top:

What would I really want from life if I were absolutely, positively certain I would get it?

Now write your answers. Don't worry about how you're going to accomplish the things on your list; we'll deal with that later. For now, focus on what you want, not on how you'll get it.

Write whatever pops into your mind. Keep your pen moving for at least two minutes. You might find it helpful to think about specific areas of your life. For example, what do you want from your work? From your home life? From your relationships? What kind of body do you want? What kind of health? What do you want from your hobbies? From your community activities? From your love life? What kind of impact would you like to have on the world? With whom would you like to associate? How would you like to be remembered?

If you run out of steam, write the same answers over and over, each time with a slightly different twist. Change a word, change a color or a size, change an adjective. Whatever you do, keep writing for at least two minutes—longer if the ideas keep flowing. Go ahead, write.

***

When you're done, take a break. Stand and stretch; go to the bathroom; take a walk; at the very least, draw a few deep breaths. When you come back, you're going to switch gears, and you'll need to feel fresh enough to take on a new challenge.

***

Priorities

You have just created your first honest-to-goodness *Wish List*. At this stage in your wishing career, it's a good idea to work on only one wish at a time, so you need to decide which item on your list you want to work on first. Here's how you go about it.

Look at the first two items on your list. Which is more important to you? In your mind, label that item your *Current Choice*. Then move to the next item on your list—the third item—and compare it with your *Current Choice*.

Which of them is more important to you? The one you prefer becomes your *Current Choice*. Now move to the next item on your list—the fourth one—and compare that with your *Current Choice*. Which of them is more important to you? The one you prefer becomes your *Current Choice*.

Repeat this process for each item on your list, comparing each one with whatever your *Current Choice* happens to be at that moment. Whenever you prefer a new item over your *Current Choice*, then that new item becomes your *Current Choice*. Continue until you've gone through your entire list.

When you come to the end of your list, the *Current Choice* that remains is the single most important item on your list. It's become your *First Choice*. You have compared it directly or indirectly with every other item and preferred it every time. Now write a "1" beside it. It's the first wish you're going to make come true, the wish you're going to work on for the rest of this book.

This method for setting priorities is called a *bubble sort*, because it allows the most important item to rise to the top of your list, the way bubbles rise to the top of a glass of champagne. I love it, because it allows you to reduce even the most complicated decisions to a series of simple "*A* or *B*" choices. You'll find it a handy tool whenever you have a choice to make, so you might want to practice it some more before you move on.

Go ahead and rank the second most important item on your Wish List. Ignore your *First Choice* because you've already ranked it. Instead, consider the remaining items, comparing only two at a time, the same way you worked through the list the first time. When you're done with the second pass, you will have selected your *Second Choice*—the second most important item on your list. Put a "2" beside it. Repeat the process to discover your *Third Choice*, your *Fourth Choice*, and so on until you've ranked the top ten items on your list.

Tough choices

What happens when you can't make up your mind between *A* or *B*? Assume for the moment that you can't have both; either it's one or none. Ask yourself, what would it feel like living without *A*? Listen to your answer. Then ask yourself, what it would feel like living without *B*? If a little voice inside you says it would be easier to live without one than to live without the other, take the hint. You've made your decision.

When you absolutely, positively can't decide between two alternatives, flip a coin. I'm serious. If you really can't choose between them, then it doesn't matter which one you choose, does it? They must be pretty close to equal, so why not make it easy on yourself?

If you do make a decision by flipping a coin, don't be surprised if you hear a little voice inside that says you made the wrong choice. Perhaps your options weren't as equal as you thought. That's OK, you can always change your mind. At least the coin-flip got you off the fence.

Remember, at this point all you're doing is establishing priorities. You aren't discarding any options. You're just choosing which wish to work on first, then second, then third. Once you've made that decision, you simply carry out your wishes in the order of their importance to you.

But first, you must decide if they're worth the price.

2

Are You Willing
To Pay The Price?

Take whatever you want, said God, but pay for it.
——*Spanish Proverb*

At a cocktail party one evening, a famous pianist gave a recital. Afterward, her hostess said, "I would give anything to be able to play like you."

The pianist looked at her thoughtfully for a moment and replied, "No you wouldn't."

The hostess, surprised and embarrassed in front of her guests, said, "I most certainly would."

The pianist shook her head. "You would love to play as I play now, but you are not willing to practice eight hours a day for twenty years to learn how to play that way."

There was silence for a moment. The guests stared into their plates. But there was no debate. They knew the pianist was right. The hostess was bluffing. She wanted to *be* a concert pianist, but she wasn't willing to pay the price to *become* one.

Every wish has its price. You can have anything you want if you are willing to pay that price. The price may be in dollars and cents, or it may be in hours of labor. It may be in the effort you expend to master a skill, or it may be in what you have to give up in order to get what you want. Whatever the price turns out to be, you have to pay full retail—you can't bargain with fate.

Your willingness to pay the price is what gives you the power to cause your wish to come true. If you are 100% willing to pay the price, then you are 100% likely to succeed. If you are 50% willing to pay the price, then you are 50% likely to succeed. It's a simple matter of cause and effect. The price is the cause; the wish is the effect. Pay the price, and your wish will come true.

A compelling reason to pay the price

Take a look at the *First Choice* from your Wish List. Think about its price. Will it cost you weeks, or months, or years of hard work? Will it require financial sacrifice? Will it mean less time with your family? Less time watching TV? Less time with your hobby, or playing golf, or puttering around the house? Why are you willing to pay that price? What reasons do you have to make that wish come true?

The people who are most successful at making their wishes come true are the ones who have the most compelling reasons to do so. Instead of trying to psyche yourself into paying an exorbitant price for a wish, choose a wish that's worth the price. Choose a wish that compels you to make it come true.

If your *First Choice* doesn't compel you, choose another

wish. Go to your *Second Choice* or your *Third Choice.* Redo your Wish List if you have to. Brainstorm new ideas and set new priorities until you choose a wish that compels you to pay the price, a wish that makes it more than worth your while to overcome every obstacle that will stand in your way. Choose a wish that is so compelling, you refuse to settle for less. You're not going to get very far until you do.

What price is too high?

Choose a wish for what it will make of you to achieve it. Don't be afraid to set your sights too high. The greater the wish, the greater you have to become to make that wish come true. And that's the real payoff. It's not what you achieve that brings joy and fulfillment; it's the person you must become in order to achieve it.

That's why it takes effort to make your magic lamp work. If all you had to do were to snap your fingers to get anything you want, you would never have to develop your potential. You would never have to become more than what you are. But by insisting that the way to earn your wish is to become the kind of person for whom such a wish is possible, the universe gives you one of the greatest gifts of all: *growth.*

Along with this gift comes a warning: Beware any wish that turns you into someone you don't want to be. That price is too high. No wish is worth sacrificing your values, your character, or your integrity. No wish is worth losing the only things worth having. If a wish forces you to become less of a person than you want to be, it's not worth the price.

3

Make Your Wish Presentable

Wishing gets a lot of bad press. As kids we're told, "If wishes were horses beggars would ride". What a crock! If beggars knew how to wish, they could charter a limousine.

Wishing has been at the heart of human accomplishment since our ancestors first dropped from the trees and began to pad along the path toward civilization. Wishing is the most powerful force at our command. But most of us don't know it exists, let alone how to command it.

The secret is this: Don't just make a wish; make it *presentable*. The power of your wish comes from the way you present it to your conscious and subconscious. If you present it effectively, you will harness the Genie-like power of your mind to cause your wish to come true. If you present it ineffectively, your mind will shrug it off as just another one of those good intentions, ill-timed and unachievable.

Below are eleven steps that will help you make your wish so presentable that it will feel only natural to make it come true. As you read about these steps, apply each one to the wish you've decided to work on first.

Step 1:   *Write it.*

If you think your wish is fixed so clearly in your mind that you don't have to put it on paper, you're kidding yourself. Write it, or kiss it good-bye. When you write your wish, you give it the kind of clarity, focus, and urgency that you can't give it any other way. You hang it out there in the world right in front of your eyes. You turn it into something real, something that stares back at you from the page and dares you to make it come true.

If you want to make your wish come true, write it down. If you don't, then don't. If it's not written, then it's not a wish—period.

Step 2:   *Be specific.*

A presentable wish is specific down to the last detail. When you can picture precisely what you want—when you can feel it, hear it, touch it, smell it, and taste it—that's specific.

The more specific you are, the better your chances for getting what you want. If you want money, how much money? By when? If you want a new house, what kind of house? Where? How many rooms? If you want a better job, in what field? At what pay? For what company? If you want a richer relationship, with whom? What will it feel like? Sound like? Look like?

When you make your wish specific, you give yourself a host of powerful advantages:

A.   *You can track your progress.*

If you don't know what you want, how will you know when you get it? For that matter, how do you know you don't already have it?

B.   *You avoid ambiguity.*

If you say, "I wish for either *A* or *B*", then your mind can't tell which alternative you want it to focus on, so it won't focus on either. But if you concentrate on a single specific wish, you free your mind to act without restraint or confusion.

C.   *You avoid unintended results.*

Vague wishes can be dangerous because they can be granted in unintended ways. For example, if you wish for "more freedom at work" you might find yourself fired. If you wish to "lose weight" you might find yourself with a serious illness, one symptom of which is weight loss. If you wish for "lots of money" you might find yourself the beneficiary of a large life-insurance policy, but the person you love the most had to die for you to collect it. Wish for exactly what you want, and you won't find yourself with what you don't want.

D.   *You focus your brain power.*

Have you ever noticed that you tend to pay attention to the things you're interested in? You buy a new car, and you begin to notice how many other people are driving the same car. You fall in love with a redhead, and you begin to notice how many other people have red hair. You read a book about nature, and you begin to notice the sunsets and the songbirds, though both have been there all along.

When you're specific about what you want, you alert your brain to notice all the people, information, and resources that can help you cause your wish to come true. Everywhere you look, you discover helpful coincidences—what the rest of the world calls *luck*—but these are coincidences you have made possible by being aware of exactly what you want. The more specific you are, the more luck you will create.

Step 3:   Set a deadline.

A wish without a deadline is just an idle daydream, with no beginning, and no end. A deadline imparts a sense of urgency, the way you feel when you're about to leave town and have lots to get done. But a deadline isn't meant to make you panic, it's meant to make you focus. Don't wear it like a straitjacket. If you find you're going to miss a deadline, go ahead and change it. Be comfortable with it. But keep your eye on it. If you want to make your wish come true, know exactly what you're shooting for—and when.

Step 4:   Make it something you can measure.

You can be winning and think you're losing because you aren't keeping score. Measurement is your way of keeping score. Measurement lets you see how much progress you have already made and how far you have to go. If you can't measure your wish, you won't know when you've made it come true.

Some wishes are easy to measure, like making a certain amount of money or losing a certain amount of weight. But how do you wish for things that aren't measurable, like a better marriage, or a more satisfying job, or a sense of inner peace? It's easy; just turn those wishes into something you can measure: specific actions.

For example, suppose your wish is to have a better marriage. To turn this immeasurable wish into something you can measure, ask yourself these questions:

1.   *What specific changes can I make in the way I act toward my partner in order to improve our marriage?*

2.   *Will I make these changes all at once or gradually?*

3.   *By when will I have completed them?*

Once you have identified specific measurable actions you can take to improve your marriage, you can phrase your wish in terms of these actions. For instance, instead of wishing for a better marriage, which you can't measure, you might wish to rub your partner's back a couple of nights a week. You might wish to vacuum the house once a month instead of letting your partner do all the housework. You might wish to cut the grass every other week instead of letting your partner do all the yard work. You might wish to take the kids to soccer practice on Saturday mornings so your partner can sleep late. You might wish to take out the garbage, or wrap the birthday presents, or clean up after a dinner party—anything to lighten the load on your partner and sweeten the relationship.

The same approach applies to wishing for a state of mind, such as happiness, joy, or contentment. You can't measure these things, so wish instead for the specific actions that will lead to the state of mind you want.

For example, if you wish to feel inner peace, and you feel it most when you're on a camping trip, wish to spend more time camping. If you wish to feel fulfilled, and you feel it most when you're performing community service, wish to spend more time serving your community. If you wish to feel happy, and you feel it most when you're with your family, wish to spend more time with your family.

Wish for something you can measure, and you will consistently measure success.

Step 5:   *Wish only for what you can control.*

A wish is about what you do, and you alone, because that's the only thing you can control. There's no room in your wish for what you want anyone else to think, do, or feel, because you can't make those things happen. Concentrate instead on the things you can make happen.

For instance, you can't wish to be loved, but you can wish to be loving. You can't wish for a heartthrob to go to dinner with you, but you can wish for courage to ask that person to dinner. You can't wish for a customer to buy, but you can wish for the guts to ask for the sale. You can't wish for someone else to make you happy, but you can wish to spend more time doing the things that make you happy.

If you wish for what you can control, success will be in your hands. If you wish for something you can't control, success will always be in the hands of others.

Step 6:   Wish for what you want, not what you don't want.

Your mind moves you toward what you think about. If you think about what you want, you'll move toward it. If you think about what you don't want, you'll move toward that instead.

Rather than saying, *"I wish I wasn't broke"*, tell yourself, *"I choose to have $100,000 in the bank."*

Rather than saying, *"I wish I wasn't fat"*, tell yourself, *"I choose to lose thirty pounds."*

Rather than saying, *"I wish I wasn't stupid"*, tell yourself, *"I choose to educate myself."*

Rather than saying, *"I wish I didn't slice my tee shot"*, tell yourself, *"I choose to hit my tee shot straight as an arrow."*

Rather than saying, *"I wish I wasn't so lonely"*, tell yourself, *"I choose to make some friends."*

Ask for what you want, and you'll get it. Ask for what you don't want, and you'll be stuck with that instead.

Step 7:   Begin your wish with "I choose".

The real secret to success is not self-discipline; it's choosing to succeed. The moment you make a choice, you eliminate all the doubt and hesitation that exist when you're trying to make up your mind. Instead of worrying about what to do, you just do it. You throw a little switch in your brain that commands you to do whatever it takes to carry out your decision. You summon all the powers of your body and mind to execute your choice.

A wish is a choice set in motion. The most effective way to set a choice in motion is to begin a wish with the words *"I choose"*. These words then transform your wish into a powerful command to carry out whatever you have chosen to do. Whenever you say *"I choose"*, you choose success.

Step 8: Make it emotional.

Your wish should include an emotional payoff so you can use the power of that emotion to help you cause your wish to come true. For instance, if your wish is to improve your marriage, you might say, "I choose to *lovingly* help my partner with the chores". If your wish is to get up each morning at six, to give yourself some personal time before you go to work, you might say, "I choose to *cheerfully* rise each morning at six." If your wish is to increase company revenues by 50%, you might say, "I choose to *joyfully* increase company revenues by 50%".

I can go into a lot of psychological mumbo jumbo about why this is important, but instead of telling you about it, I would rather show you. Play along with me and you'll see what I mean.

Choose an emotion you would like to feel when you make your wish come true. Now, add that word to your wish. For instance, if joy is what you want to feel, and your wish is "I choose to find a new job," change your wish so that it reads, "I choose to *joyfully* find a new job". Then say your wish aloud, with the emotion-word included, and make sure you feel the emotion when you say it. If you're saying "cheerful," *feel* cheerful. If you're saying "happy," *feel* happy. If you're saying "triumphant," *feel* triumphant.

Now remove the emotion-word and repeat your wish

without any emotion at all. Notice how flat it feels. It's no longer charged with passion or spirit. Your wish is like an electrical appliance, and your emotions are like a wall socket. You'll get a lot more done if you stay plugged in.

When you build an emotional payoff into your wish you tend to work harder at it because you enjoy it more. The harder you work, the more likely you are to make your wish come true. Before you know it, you'll enjoy the work as much as you enjoy the results. From that point on, the results will take care of themselves.

Step 9:   Be brief.

Less is more. The shorter your wish, the greater the emotional impact. A single short sentence is perfect. To keep your wish brief, act as if each word costs you $10,000.

Step 10:   Believe in it.

Why would a gardener take the trouble to plant a seed, water it, fertilize it, and tend it—perhaps for weeks—before seeing any return at all on the effort? Because he believes the seed will grow into something worth the effort. Perhaps it will turn into a flower, or a fruit, or a useful vegetable. Whatever the expected result, the expectation must come before the result. The only gardens we bother to tend are the ones we believe will grow.

When you make a wish, you have to believe you will succeed, or else you won't be willing to make the effort. With belief comes action. With action comes results. Without belief there is neither action nor results.

Step 11:   Take immediate action.

The final step you need to take to make your wish presentable is to send your brain the most powerful message of all—*act now*. If you don't, you'll fall prey to the Law of Diminishing Intent: the more time that passes before you act, the less likely you'll be to act.

Before you get up from your chair, do something to put your wish into action. Make a phone call, create a plan, read a useful article in a newspaper or magazine, write a letter. Do something to get the ball rolling. *Do anything.* The important thing is to take some kind of action right now, before you lose the moment, and with it your chance to make your wish come true.

Make your wish presentable.

If you haven't already been doing so as we've gone along, take the time now to go back and make your wish presentable. Take it through each of the eleven steps. Write it. Make it specific. Make it measurable. Make it all the things it needs to be to come true. Then take immediate action to start you on your way.

If you've come this far and still don't know what to wish for, then make that your first wish: *Wish to know what to wish for.* Make it an official wish. Make it presentable. Take immediate action. Do this now, and you will launch yourself on a lifetime of making your wishes come true.

4

Plan

You know what to wish for. You have committed yourself to pay the price. You have made your wish presentable. Now you need to create a LAMP Plan that will cause your wish to come true.

A LAMP Plan is nothing more than your wish broken into steps so compellingly small that you can't wait to get started on the first one, then the next, and then the one after that, until before you know it you've completed your wish.

Your LAMP Plan is a bridge from thinking to doing. It translates your wish from an idea into the actions necessary to turn that idea into reality.

A good plan motivates you to complete even the most minor details because it drapes each one in the larger purpose. When you work any step of the plan, you feel like you're working the whole plan so every step is worth your best effort.

But the magic of your plan is not in the details, it's in the freedom those details give you. Freedom from the distraction of worrying about what to do next. Freedom to focus all your energy and attention on the single step at hand, knowing that every step you complete takes you that much closer to where you want to go. Freedom to try, because you know exactly what you need to do to guarantee success. A good plan sets your mind at ease and your body in motion. It removes confusion, uncertainty, and doubt so you can concentrate on getting the job done.

Brainstorming a plan

When I create a plan, I start with my end in mind and then brainstorm how to get there from here. At the top of a piece of paper, I write this question: *What steps do I need to take to* _____ *?* All I have to do is to fill in the blank, ask myself the question, and then write my answers.

Lets make up an example. Suppose your wish is to become Director of Finance for ACME Emporium. At the top of a piece of paper you would write this question: *What steps do I need to take to become Director of Finance at ACME Emporium?* Then you would write your answers. They might look like this:

1. Lobby my friends to see if any of them have contacts at ACME Emporium.
2. Identify the specific person I should approach at ACME Emporium.
3. Line up the references most likely to get me this job.
4. Update my resume.
5. Research ACME Emporium.

Once you have listed as many steps as you can think

of, you arrange them in the order in which it makes the most sense to execute them:

1. Research ACME Emporium.
2. Lobby my friends to see if any of them have contacts at ACME Emporium.
3. Identify the specific person I should approach at ACME Emporium.
4. Update my resume.
5. Line up references most likely to get me this job.

Then you break the larger steps into smaller steps. For example, *Step 4* might look like this:

Step 4.   Update my resume.

    A.   Read a book about writing resumes.
    B.   Attend a seminar about writing resumes.
    C.   Ask a friend for advice.
    D.   Write the first draft.
    E.   Run the first draft by some friends.
    F.   Complete my resume.
    G.   Make as many copies as I need.

Some of these steps, in turn, might be broken into even smaller steps, and these into smaller steps still. The idea is to keep breaking them down until you create steps so small that they appear inviting to you. You want to feel confident that you can go from one step to the next without undue hardship. No step should be so intimidating that you can't face it, or else when you reach it the whole process will grind to a halt.

After you've broken down one major step this way, repeat the process for each of the others, until each large step is reduced to a series of manageable tasks. You will then have a list of all the steps necessary to take you from where you are to where you want to go. Once you look at this list and realize how easily you can handle everything on it, you will begin to understand how simple it is to make your wish come true. It's like building a ladder and leaning it against a towering tree. When you're done you can stand back, admire your handiwork, and say with conviction, "Now I *know* I can climb it."

Deadlines

We've already seen that you don't have a wish until you have a deadline. The same holds true for a plan—without a deadline it's just a fantasy. The purpose of a deadline is to make you feel a sense of urgency. It lets you know how serious you are about making your wish come true. It switches on the light at the end of the tunnel, so you quicken your pace to reach it.

Set reasonable deadlines. If you want to get a new job, give yourself at least six months, not six weeks. If you want to double your sales, give yourself a year, not a month. If you want to achieve financial independence and you're starting from scratch, give yourself a decade, not a year. A deadline is designed to make you focus, not to make you panic.

When I began *The Magic Lamp*, I set a deadline of seven months to complete it. Seven months later I was delighted with my progress, but I was barely half done. I thought I had let myself down until I realized that my only crime was to underestimate how long it would take me to write the kind of book I wanted to write. Instead of beating myself up, I simply reset my deadline for twelve months rather than seven. In the end, the book took fifteen months—more than twice as long as I had originally planned. But I finished it.

The advantage of setting a deadline is that you fix your wish in time, not just in your mind. You begin to plan your life around it, the same way you plan around any other important event. Your wish becomes real, like an appointment, or a holiday, or a business trip you've scheduled for next month. The more real your wish becomes, the more convinced you become that you can make your wish come true.

One frosty afternoon during the winter before I completed *The Magic Lamp*, I remember thinking ahead to the vacation my family and I were planning to spend at the beach the coming summer. I was reviewing where I would be with my various projects by the time we left for vacation when an interesting thought struck me: *The Magic Lamp* would be finished. By then I would be working with my publisher to schedule book signings, publicity interviews, speaking engagements. And I would be halfway through my next book. These events seemed as real to me as if they were already memories.

Except that I didn't have a publisher. I hadn't scheduled any book signings, publicity interviews, or speaking engagements. I hadn't even finished my book. But I had finished my plan. I had set deadlines. The instant I began to schedule around those deadlines, my wish became as real to me as if I had already completed it. In that moment, I knew for certain that I would complete it, just as surely as I knew that I would be lounging on the beach come August.

Once you fix your wish in time, it will feel like the most natural thing in the world to complete it in time. That's the power of a deadline.

Milestones

Milestones are intermediate targets designed to keep you on track toward your main deadline. They help you make continuous progress over time, so you don't have to accomplish everything at the last moment.

For example, suppose in November you decide to lose thirty pounds by the time you leave for vacation the following July. To help you meet your deadline, you might set a milestone of losing a pound every week. If you meet each weekly milestone, then by July you will have lost all thirty pounds. If you miss a milestone or two, you still have time to take corrective action—before it's too late.

Scheduling

Once you've listed the steps you need to take to make your wish come true, and you've set milestones to keep you on track toward your deadline, you need to transfer both the steps and the milestones to your daily schedule. Scheduling bridges the gap between planning and doing. It's the difference between a good intention and an appointment. Instead of saying to an old friend, "Let's have lunch sometime," scheduling lets you say, "Let's have lunch next Tuesday at 1 PM."

If you've ever used a pocket scheduler, you already know how to schedule the steps and the milestones of your LAMP Plan. Simply enter each step into your scheduler the same way you would enter a meeting, or a lunch date, or an appointment with your doctor. You don't have to schedule the entire plan all at once, just the next week or two. Then if a step takes longer than expected, or your schedule is disrupted in some other way, you won't have as much to reschedule.

When you schedule a step on your calendar, you are making an appointment with yourself. Keep it. Treat it like an appointment with the most important person in the world. It is.

Take yourself seriously. If you don't, who will? Take yourself as seriously as you want the rest of the world to take you. After all, why should anyone else treat you better than you treat yourself? If you want other people to keep their appointments with you, keep your appointments with yourself. If you want other people to be there when you need them, be there for yourself.

The Limiting Factor

The *limiting factor* is the bottleneck that governs how rapidly you can make your wish come true. For a LAMP Plan to be successful, it must be designed to overcome this limiting factor. Consider these examples:

Bill is a middle-aged stockbroker whose wish is to get back into shape by exercising at six each morning before he heads to the office. But he hates to drag himself out of bed that early, so every morning he invents a new excuse to sleep late, and every morning he skips his workout. Sleeping late is the limiting factor in his plan. If he's ever going to shape up, he first has to get up.

Polly is a computer salesperson who plans to double her sales in the next year, but she is terrified of prospecting. Fear is her limiting factor. She will have to deal with this fear before she can increase her prospecting enough to double her sales.

Manuel is an unhappy accountant who desperately wants to find a new job, but he can't find the time to look for one. Time management is his limiting factor. He has to learn how to fit job-hunting into his already overloaded schedule, or he will be stuck in his current job until he retires—or gets fired.

The distinguishing characteristic of a limiting factor is that once you overcome it, everything else falls into place. If Bill develops the habit of bouncing out of bed at six each morning, he will soon be able to work himself into shape. If Polly learns to enjoy prospecting instead of fearing it, her sales will shoot off the chart. If Manuel learns how to manage his time, he will soon find all the time he needs to look for a new job.

Now consider your wish. What is it that most limits your progress? What factor, once changed, will make everything else fall into place? It might be a habit you need to change, like it was with Bill; or a skill you need to acquire, like it was with Manuel; or it might be your way of looking at the world, like it was with Polly. Once you have pinpointed the limiting factor in your wish, design your LAMP Plan to overcome it.

When I decided to change careers and become a writer, after twenty years in the world of business, I found myself facing a classic limiting factor: I didn't want to write. I thought about writing. I read books about it. I dreamed about being a world-famous author. But the writing itself was a dreadful chore.

Rather than force myself to do something I didn't want to do, I focused my LAMP Plan on learning how to enjoy the process of writing. Once I accomplished that, everything else fell into place.

You will discover the same thing. When you identify the limiting factor for your wish and gear your LAMP Plan to overcome it, the rest of your wish will fall into place.

Schedule progress reports

Once you've listed the steps of your Lamp Plan and scheduled them on your calendar, you need to schedule regular progress reports to see how you're coming along.

A progress report is like looking out the window while you're riding a train. By observing what you're passing, you can tell whether or not the train is going in the right direction. But if you aren't paying attention, you can come to the end of the line and find yourself in the wrong city.

To schedule progress reports, estimate how long it will take you to complete your wish and divide that time into regular intervals. If your wish will take a year, for example, make a progress report to yourself every month. If your wish will take a month, make a progress report every week. Include these reports in your LAMP Plan. Then schedule the dates in your calendar, the same way you schedule the other steps of your plan.

When the time comes to make a progress report, ask yourself these questions:

1. *Have I met the milestones I had planned to meet since my last progress report?*
2. *Do I need to change my plan to reach my milestones?*
3. *Do I need to change my milestones?*

Reality changes constantly. Your plan may need to change with it. If you find that you need to make changes, make them. If you need to revise your plan, revise it. That's what a progress report is all about.

End your plan with your next wish

In 1969, Buzz Aldrin was one of the first two men to walk on the moon. When he returned to earth, having achieved his life's ambition, he had a nervous breakdown. It's not enough to walk on the moon; you have to figure out what comes next.

The human mind is a problem-solving tool. If you don't give it a problem to solve, it will create one. If you don't give it work to do, it will make work. Or it may prolong what it's currently working on—it may slow down the progress on your wish—just to keep itself occupied.

You can avoid this by having another wish queued up and ready to go. I don't mean you have to jump from one wish right into another. Go ahead and celebrate when you complete a wish. Take a vacation, recharge your batteries. But know what comes next. Know that when it's time to get back to work, you have meaningful work to get back to. No LAMP Plan is complete until you've included that final step: your next wish.

You are already a planner, whether you like it or not.

Many people tell me they don't believe in planning because it takes the spontaneity out of life. So I ask them where they're going on their next vacation. They light up like kids on Christmas morning and launch into the details: where they're going, when they'll leave, how long they'll be gone, what they intend to do. There's a name for this kind of information—it's called a plan.

Plans work. You've been proving that all your life. Have you ever taken a vacation and found yourself a thousand miles from where you intended to go? Have you ever made it halfway to your destination, then given up and come home? When you're on vacation, you know where you want to go, how to get there, when you'll leave, how long you'll stay—and you're determined to complete the journey.

What if your life worked the same way? It will, if you plan your wishes the way you plan your vacations. Take your wishes as seriously as you take your vacations, and you might just turn your whole life into a vacation.

L<u>A</u>MP Process
Step Two:

<u>A</u>ct

5

Inertia

A wish is a self-fulfilled prophecy.
—*Alan Ellis*

A plan gives your wish form; action gives it life. The first step in the LAMP Process is to lock onto your wish and plan to make it come true. The second step is to take the action called for in your plan.

When you act, you set causes in motion. When you set causes in motion, you are rewarded with effects. When you take action, you make a giant leap from *thinking* your wish to *living* your wish. You change yourself from a dreamer to a doer. To make that leap, you need to overcome one of the greatest forces in nature: *inertia*.

While I was still in college, I decided that I wanted to become a writer, but for the next dozen years I did everything but write. I worked as a salesman, helped to raise my family, cut the lawn, took out the trash, hung the Christmas lights, and watched my favorite sitcoms on TV. When I reached spitting distance of forty, I realized that I was going to have to call my bluff—start writing or give up my dream of being a writer. I decided to stick with my dream, but that still left me with the same problem: How was I going to get myself to write?

Then I remembered something I learned in high school physics: the law of inertia. A body in motion tends to remain in motion; a body at rest tends to remain at rest. I began to wonder if inertia applied to human behavior the way it applied to the behavior of comets streaking past the sun. What if my problem was simply inertia? What if all I had to do was to turn myself from a body at rest to a body in motion?

I decided to find out. I made a commitment to myself to write something every day. It didn't matter how little I wrote: a sentence or two if I wanted, or even a single word if that's all I could muster. But no matter how busy I was, or how distracted, or how tired, I had to write something every day. I promised myself I would try this for thirty days and see what happened.

It worked, and I learned one of the great lessons of my life: Inertia is the single greatest barrier to success. It's also the easiest to overcome. All you have to do is to act. Any action you take, no matter how trivial, will do the trick.

The easier you make it on yourself to act, the easier it is to overcome inertia. For instance, I made it so easy on myself to write that I no longer had any reason not to. Instead of making a big production out of it, I made it as small a production as I could. I gave myself permission to do nothing more than to pound out a few keystrokes on my word processor.

That simple act of typing was all I needed to overcome inertia. With my first keystroke, I turned myself from a body at rest into a body in motion. Once in motion, the most natural thing for me to do was to continue in motion and keep writing. So I did. I would sit to write a single sentence and stand having completed an entire page.

You can overcome your own inertia the same way. Think small. Instead of trying to complete your wish in a single day, focus on a single step, the smallest step you can think of. The moment you take action—any action—you will conquer inertia. You will become a body in motion and will tend to stay in motion. The most natural thing in the world will be for you to take the next step, and then the next, until you've completed your wish.

This simple but profound principle allowed me to breathe new life not only into my writing but into my day job as a salesperson. For years I used to dread the dozens of phone calls I had to make every day. I kept putting them off, and they kept piling up, making me dread them even more. Everything changed when I learned the secret of inertia.

I committed myself to make at least one phone call the moment I got to the office every morning. I didn't have to make twenty calls, or ten, or even five. I just had to make one before I did anything else—before I said good morning to my associates, before I stopped by the water cooler, before I went to the bathroom. The act of dialing that first call transformed me from a body at rest to a body in motion. Once I was a body in motion, it felt only natural to make a second call, then a third. Before I knew it, I was on top of my phone calls instead of having my phone calls on top of me.

I cured more than my phone problem. My whole day became more productive. From the moment I arrived at work, I became a body in motion and tended to stay in motion. A body in motion gets a lot more work done than does a body at rest.

The First Step

A journey of a thousand miles begins with a single step. Your LAMP Plan, no matter how simple or how complex, begins the same way.

Your *First Step* is the one that overcomes inertia, the one that transforms you from a body at rest to a body in motion. Take that step and you have the momentum you need to carry you to the next step. That's all you have to worry about. You don't need enough momentum to complete your whole plan; all you need is enough to complete your next step. Then that momentum will carry you to the next step, then the next, then the next after that, until you complete your wish.

The secret of that First Step is to make it so simple, so unintimidating, that you give yourself no reason to resist it. For instance, if your wish calls for you to become a concert pianist, tell yourself you're just going to practice a few notes. If you want to look for a new job, tell yourself you're just going to update the first line of your resume. If you want to become a movie star, tell yourself you're just going to watch a movie to see how the pros do it. If you want to run for President of the United States, jot down the first three things you'll do once you're in office.

You can never finish what you never start. The easier you make it on yourself to take the First Step, the greater your chances to make it to the last step, the one that completes your plan and makes your wish come true.

There are many first steps

There are many other "first steps" on your journey, as

many as there are stops along the way. Whenever you pause in carrying out your wish—for a phone call, for dinner, to go to work at your day job, to take your summer vacation—when you try to resume, you'll find yourself once more in the deadening grip of inertia. Your natural tendency, once stopped, will be to remain stopped. You'll have to find a way to get started all over again.

Think of the smallest and easiest thing you can do to get yourself restarted, and then do it. You don't have to begin at the beginning, you can begin at the point of least resistance. It's like climbing a hill. You don't have to start at the bottom, where the grade looks the steepest. You can start in the middle, or near the top. Then it won't seem so difficult to begin.

Once you do begin, you'll turn yourself into a body in motion and momentum will take care of the rest. Then you'll find how much easier it is to make your wishes come true when the law of inertia is working for you instead of against you.

6

Habits

The easiest actions for us to take are the ones we perform out of habit. The easiest way to grant yourself a wish is to make a habit out of the actions you must take to cause that wish to come true.

You can create new habits the same way you created all of your existing habits—through repetition. Every habit you've got you formed by doing something over and over again until it became second nature. To form a new habit, all you have to do is to apply the same principle.

Practice

When I was in high school, I must have tried three or four times to teach myself how to play the guitar. I would open my song book to a Bob Dylan tune and try to place my fingers on the strings the way the book showed me. I would struggle with the chords and my sore fingertips for two or three days and then quit. A year later I would be back at it: same songs, same guitar, same result.

In college, I met a music major who agreed to teach me how to play guitar, on one condition: I had to practice at least twenty minutes a day for thirty days in a row, to get myself into the habit. If I wasn't willing to practice, he wasn't willing to teach. I agreed to his terms, and after thirty days I was playing the guitar.

My teacher taught me an important lesson about the guitar, but he taught me an even more important lesson about life: In thirty days you can turn almost anything into a habit, if you practice it for a few minutes every day.

Suppose, for example, that you wish to take a walk each morning to work yourself into shape, but you're having trouble giving up your morning routine—your habit—of reading the newspaper. What you need is a new habit to replace the old one. For thirty days, practice walking each morning instead of reading the paper. At first, you may feel uncomfortable because your old habit still has hold of you. But by the second or third week, you'll begin to find it more natural to walk each morning than to read the paper. After a month of this, you'll find that walking has become your new habit.

If you try this and find that the new habit isn't taking hold, it's probably because you skipped a day. That won't work. You can't afford to skip even a single day. If you do, your momentum will drop to zero, and you'll have to start over again. It's like hitting the brakes when you're driving your car up an icy hill. You can try to get moving again from where you stop, but your best bet is to roll back to the bottom and start over. During that first thirty days, if you miss even a single day of practice, reset your thirty-day clock to Day One and start from the beginning. The next time around, practice every day. By the thirtieth day, you will have given yourself a new habit.

Internal practice

When we think of practice, we usually think of what I call *external practice*, the kind you do with your body. But there is a second kind of practice, one that is equally useful when it comes to developing a new habit and far easier to perform. I call it *internal practice* because you do it with your mind.

You have been conducting your own internal practice sessions since you were a kid. Remember when you had to a give a report before the whole class and you rehearsed it over and over again in your mind? Or when you wanted to ask someone out and you rehearsed just what you were going to say and how you were going to say it? If you were an athlete, you probably pictured winning. If you were in drama, you pictured yourself performing flawlessly in front of an auditorium full of people. If you were in the band, you imagined yourself hitting all the right notes.

All of these are examples of what psychologists call *visualization*. That's just a fancy word for practicing with your mind instead of your body. The latest research into visualization proves that your mind can't tell much of a difference between an activity you visualize and one you actually perform. This suggests that you can benefit nearly as much from practicing with your mind as you can from practicing with your body.

For example, researchers at Ohio State University divided a group of basketball players into three teams. Each team shot some foul shots, and the researchers recorded the scores. Then for the next month, the first team practiced shooting foul shots for half an hour every day. The second team visualized themselves shooting foul shots for half an hour every day but never actually shot any. The third team neither practiced foul shooting nor visualized themselves doing it.

When the month was up, the researchers retested the shooting skills of each team. The third team, the ones who neither practiced nor visualized practicing, showed no improvement at all. The first team, the ones who actually practiced foul shooting, improved their results by 28%. The second team, the ones who visualized themselves shooting foul shots but never shot any, improved by 27%—virtually the same amount as the first team, without ever touching a basketball.

How can your mind have such a powerful effect over your body? We don't really know the answer; we just know that it does. And you know it, too, from your own experience. Have you ever bolted awake in the middle of a nightmare, dripping with sweat and shaking with fear? It was all in your mind, but try to explain that to your body. Of course, a nightmare is unintentional. Just imagine what you can accomplish when you put your mind to it.

To practice visualization, try this simple exercise. You'll need to be limber enough to do some twisting and turning, so you might want to warm up and stretch a little before you proceed. (If you have a bad back, skip this exercise and go to the next one). You'll need at least an arm's length of space around you.

Step 1:   Stand and extend your arms out to your sides, like you're an airplane ready for take off. Point your index fingers. Notice what your right index finger is pointing at. Now twist at the waist as far as you can (keeping your arms pointed out to your sides) and notice what that same finger is pointing at when you can't twist any farther. Twist back to center, drop your arms, take a couple of deep breaths, and relax.

Step 2: Now close your eyes. In your mind's eye, perform the twisting exercise you just completed, but this time, see yourself twisting farther, past where you stopped before. Remember what your index finger was pointing at when you stopped the first time? This time around, picture what your finger will be pointing at as it twists past that first stopping point.

Step 3: Open your eyes and perform for real what you just pictured in your mind.

Chances are, you twisted farther the second time because you pictured yourself doing so. You practiced it in your mind; then your brain interpreted your mental practice as if it were a real experience. When you executed your second twist, you were able to perform with your body what you had already performed with your mind.

Here's another exercise: Extend your arms straight out in front of you, perfectly level with one another and parallel to the ground. Close your eyes and imagine that someone has just placed a pail full of water in your left hand, and you're straining with all your might to support the pail and keep your arm level. Into your right hand, someone slips a string. Tied to the end of the string is a large helium-filled balloon. As the balloon floats upward, it gently pulls your right arm along with it, while your left arm is struggling with the pail of water that seems to grow heavier by the second.

Now open your eyes. Chances are, your arms are no longer level. When your mind painted its pictures—the pail of water in one hand and the balloon in the other—your body had no choice but to respond. That's the power of visualization.

Pre-memory

The term *visualization* is misleading. Internal practice is far more than seeing the appropriate pictures in your mind. You must also feel the appropriate feelings, hear the appropriate sounds, taste the appropriate tastes, and smell the appropriate smells. You need to experience your practice session in your mind as if you were actually experiencing it with your body. The more realistic you make your mental practice, the more firmly you fix the "experience" in your brain.

Sometimes a mental experience is so powerful that it feels like a memory instead of like something you just dreamed up. I call this kind of intense mental image a *pre-memory*. A pre-memory is something you "remember" before it happens, because you want to make it happen the way you've "remembered" it. You imagine the pictures, feelings, and sounds of your experience, as well as the tastes and smells if there are any, as clearly as if they have already happened.

Pre-memories are the most powerful kind of internal practice, rivaling the memories you retain from actual experience. Your mind can tell so little difference between what's real and what you've imagined that you can use pre-memories to create new habits the same way you've used actual experience to create your existing habits. All it takes is repetition.

To use pre-memories to form a new habit, just ask yourself these questions:

1. *What would I see through my own eyes if I were actually practicing my new habit?*
2. *What would I hear?*
3. *How would I feel?*

For example, suppose you want to create a new habit of reading in the evening when you get home from work, to replace your old habit of collapsing on the couch and staring at the TV. First, picture your TV. Then picture your hand reaching out to turn it off. In your mind's ear, listen to the "click" of the on-off switch, and hear the dialogue die in mid-sentence, leaving only silence.

Now picture your hand picking up a good book. Picture your home as you move through it to find a seat in your favorite chair or sofa. How would the room look around you? How would you feel as you settle into a comfortable position in your chair?

Picture your hands opening the book. How would the pages look? How would they feel? What sound would they make? To deepen your experience, ask yourself this question:

How would I feel if I really were enjoying this new habit?

Internal practice is an effective substitute for external practice, but the best way to create a new habit is to use both. Practice your new habit externally at least once a day. Then practice it internally at least once a day. If you do both, you will learn your new habit more quickly than you ever thought possible.

Affirmation

There is a second kind of internal practice that seems so simple it's hard to believe it really works, but it does. And you've been practicing it since you were old enough to speak.

Though we hate to admit it, we all talk to ourselves. More importantly, we listen. Psychologists call this *affirmation*. What they mean is this: If you tell yourself something often enough, you begin to believe it.

Most of us are pretty good at affirming our shortcomings. We knock over an iced tea at a lawn party and say, *"I'm so clumsy!"* We forget to bring our briefcase to work and say, *"I'd forget my own head if it weren't screwed-on!"* We make a mistake quoting a price to a customer and say, *"I'm so lousy at math I can't even balance my own checkbook!"*

But we can affirm our strengths too. We can even affirm strengths we don't yet have, as a way of turning them into habits.

For instance, if you would like to become the kind of person who bounces out of bed every morning at six, you can tell yourself: *I love to rise each morning at six, refreshed and invigorated for the entire day.* If you're a salesperson and you want to learn to love prospecting, you can tell yourself: *I love to prospect for new customers.* If you want to develop the habit of better time management, you can tell yourself: *I love to plan my work and work my plan.*

I've used affirmations to create all sorts of useful habits. For example, I used to hate to solve problems. Whenever I encountered a problem, my habit was to duck it and hope it would go away. After forty years of hiding my head in the sand, I realized that I would never get what I wanted from life until I learned how to solve the problems that stood in my way. It wasn't enough for me just to face problems; I wanted to learn how to enjoy solving them, so I made the following contract with myself:

> For thirty days, at least ten times a day, I agree to tell myself: *I love to solve problems*. I agree to say it with the kind of heartfelt conviction that will leave no room for doubt. At the end of thirty days, if I still hate to solve problems, I will allow myself to cling to that habit for the rest of my life.

Then I went to work. The first couple of days I felt resistance. Every time I repeated my affirmation, an angry little voice in my mind would say: *Who are you trying to kid with this affirmation crap? You hate to solve problems!* I couldn't disagree with that, and I didn't want to lie to myself, so I pretended I was an actor playing the part of a character who loved to solve problems. Before I knew it, the resistance disappeared.

Within a week, I began to enjoy saying my affirmation. Within two weeks, I began to look forward to saying it. It made me feel good, as if I were lifting a massive load from my shoulders every time I said it. Often I would repeat my affirmation more than ten times just for the fun of it. I even began to laugh when I said it because saying it made me feel so good. I knew that if I could learn how to love solving problems, then I could accomplish anything. No wonder I felt giddy at the prospect!

By the end of the thirty days, I found myself looking

for problems to solve. Whenever I encountered one, I would hear myself say: *I love to solve problems!* Then I would plunge right in and solve it. My affirmation had come true, and that allowed me to make a quantum leap forward in my life.

The first step in creating an affirmation is to make certain it supports your values. If you feel it's unethical or undesirable, then it won't work (and you wouldn't want it to). The next step is to follow similar guidelines to the ones you used when you created a presentable wish. Be specific. Affirm what you want instead of what you don't want. Use the present tense. Give it intense emotional impact.

That last point is the one that counts the most. The real power of an affirmation comes from how deeply you feel it, not from how many times you say it. You want emotional content, not repetition for the sake of repetition. But how can you feel emotion about something you don't really believe?

Don't worry about whether you believe an affirmation, worry about whether you *want* to believe it. If you want to believe it—if you intensely want to believe it—and you repeat it with that same intensity, then you will soon come to believe it, the same way you've come to believe so much negative garbage about yourself. If you're going to pump yourself full of propaganda anyway, why not choose propaganda that serves a useful purpose? Just make certain that your affirmations contain emotional words like *love* and *joy*, and let yourself feel those words when you say them. Emotion is the magic ingredient that will turn your affirmations into reality.

As the days pass, you'll find it easier to move your behavior into line with your affirmation. The trick is not to force yourself, but to listen to yourself. For example, if your affirmation is: *I prefer to eat healthy food*, that doesn't mean you have to give up junk food on the spot. Listen to your affirmation. Feel it. Then gradually change your behavior when it feels right to do so. Before you know it, you'll find yourself substituting an apple for a candy bar and pasta for fried chicken. Within thirty days, you'll start to think differently about what you eat, so it will seem only natural to eat differently as well.

Schedule your practice

Schedule the date and time for your practice sessions, the same way you schedule other important appointments. Then honor your schedule. If you have trouble keeping appointments with yourself, then that's the first habit you need to change. Learn to treat an appointment with yourself the same way you would treat an appointment with the President of the United States. Even if you didn't vote for him, you probably wouldn't keep him waiting.

Thirty Day Plan

You can turn almost anything into a habit if you implement what I call a *Thirty Day Plan*. All you have to do is to decide what new habit you want to acquire and then agree to practice that habit every day for just thirty days. If in thirty days you don't like the results, quit. That's all there is to it.

Make sure you schedule each day's practice and then honor your schedule. Don't let yourself skip days because of weekends, or holidays, or illness, or because you had to go out of town. Don't accept any excuses for missing even a single day. If you do miss a day, start over.

The beauty of a Thirty Day Plan is that it minimizes your natural resistance to change. You aren't asking yourself to give up anything; you're just asking yourself to try something new for awhile. You can stand almost anything for a few days. After thirty days, if you don't like your new habit, you're free to go back to the old one. But the chances are that by then your new habit will feel more comfortable than the one it has replaced.

7

Comfort Zone

Have you ever wondered why most New Year's resolutions rarely last beyond New Year's Day? Have you ever wondered why habits are so hard to break? Have you ever wondered why even the best intentions of one moment are forgotten in the rush of the next?

At home, you probably set your thermostat to turn on the air conditioning if the temperature gets too high, say 78 degrees, or to turn on the heater if the temperature falls too low, say 68 degrees. These settings create what is known in the heating-and-cooling business as a *comfort zone*. Whenever the temperature moves beyond the zone, the thermostat automatically makes the adjustments necessary to bring it back within the zone.

The human mind works much the same way. Each of us has our own internal "comfort settings" by which we tend to operate, like the upper and lower settings of a thermostat. We regulate our behavior by these settings, the way a thermostat regulates the temperature of a room. Whenever our life falls too far below our settings or rises too far above them, our mental thermostat kicks in to bring us back within our comfort zone.

When we make a New Year's resolution or try to change an old habit, we move ourselves beyond our comfort zone. But not for long. Our mental thermostat will soon do whatever it needs to do to bring us back to where we belong. Before we know it, our good intentions are forgotten, and we're back in the same old rut. No wonder it seems so hard to change.

A wish, like a New Year's resolution, takes you beyond your comfort zone. If you want to make certain a wish comes true, you will have to adjust your comfort zone to accommodate that wish. If you don't, sooner or later you will find yourself giving up your wish and returning to your old familiar ways.

Adjusting your comfort zone

To adjust your comfort zone, you have only to change the settings in your mind, much the way you would change the settings of a thermostat to adjust the comfort zone of a room. Once you change yourself on the inside, the outside will soon catch up. Change your idea of how you should live, and you will soon change how you do live. That's the way human beings operate.

Your comfort zone is determined by the mental movies you show yourself by force of habit. To change your comfort zone, simply change your movies. Your mind will then regulate your actions according to the new settings, the way it used to regulate your actions according to the old settings.

To change your movies, think of your mind as your own private movie theater. You are the projectionist. You control the sound, the brightness, the color, even the speed at which you roll the film. You can show whatever movies you choose for as long as you choose. You can run the same movies over and over, or just your favorite scenes. If you don't like a movie you're showing, you can stop it mid-scene and show something else.

Your movies are habits, so you can change them the same way you can change any other habit—with practice. Practice a new movie for thirty days, without missing a day, and you will begin to play it automatically, the same way you used to play the old one. Keep practicing until your new movie feels as natural as the old one.

For example, suppose you decide to replace your old habit of sleeping late with a new habit of rising at 6 AM, so you have some free time to work on your wish before you head to the office. The problem is, you hate to get out of bed that early. Just thinking about your alarm going off at 6 AM fills you with dread. You can't even imagine yourself getting up.

That's because you're running the wrong movie. So run a different one. Show a movie in which you can't wait to bounce out of bed at 6 AM, energized for the whole day. Fill yourself with expectation instead of with dread. Feel the exhilaration of having the world by the tail because you've become the master of your own sleeping habits.

Watch your new movie as if you were seeing it through your own eyes, rather than as a spectator. Play the movie over and over—at least five times a day—and make doubly sure you roll it whenever you find yourself thinking about how early you have to get up the next morning.

The idea is to turn your new movie into a pre-memory, so you can roll it as easily as you used to roll the old movie. Imagine yourself getting up at 6 AM as if you already do it.

Live it in your mind. Feel your eyes popping open on time, without an alarm. Notice how wonderful it feels to bounce out of bed full of energy, ready to meet your day. Hear yourself say how great it makes you feel. Keep practicing your new movie until it feels as natural as the old movie. Keep practicing it until it becomes the movie you automatically launch each morning when it's time to get up.

Meanwhile, practice an affirmation. If you're the kind of person who likes to sleep late, the chances are you've been telling yourself that for years. So tell yourself something different. Instead of saying *I love to sleep late*, tell yourself *I love to rise at six each morning, refreshed and invigorated for the entire day*. Say it with genuine emotion, not because it's true, but because you want it to become true. Repeat it with intense emotion ten times a day for thirty days. As you do, you'll find it easier and easier to run your new movie. The easier it gets to run your new movie, the easier it gets to jump out of bed.

When you turn this new movie into a habit, you will have successfully adjusted the settings of your comfort zone. At that point, rising at 6 AM will seem like the most natural thing in the world to do, more natural than sleeping late.

When you change your comfort zone, you change your life. In junior high school, I hated to run any farther than from the TV to the refrigerator. I was also dreadfully overweight. One summer, I decided to get into shape by jogging a mile each day around a nearby track. Each afternoon, dripping sweat as I baked under the sun, I would begin my first lap around that steamy cinder track, wondering every step of the way if I could make it a whole mile. It was horrible. It was torture. It was worse than being fat. I fought myself every step, every day, until finally I gave up.

A couple of years later, in high school, I joined the cross-country team. Back on that same cinder track where I used to hate to jog a mile, under that same fiery sun, the cross-country team jogged two miles every day—*just to warm up*. And I jogged with them.

Somewhere along the line, without realizing it, I had changed the movie I was showing in my mind. I used to picture running as agony, but by the time I joined the cross-country team I had learned to picture running as fun. Once I changed the movie in my mind, my body took the change for granted. By changing the settings of my comfort zone, I changed what had been torture into nothing more than a warm-up.

When you learn how to change your comfort zone to accommodate your wishes, you'll find it the most natural thing in the world to make those wishes come true.

Discomfort

The thing to keep in mind about making any kind of change, whether it's changing a habit or changing your comfort zone, is that the process of change itself is uncomfortable. When you make a change, the chances are that at first you're going to feel some mild discomfort. That's not a symptom that something is wrong; it's a symptom that something is right. The discomfort is telling you that you're going beyond what you're accustomed to. You're attempting something that you aren't yet comfortable with because you want to become comfortable with it. You're stretching the old you in a new direction that will eventually produce a new and better you.

That's called growth. And growth is what life is all

about. Somebody once said that if you aren't growing, you're dying. In a strictly physical sense, that's true. Once our cells stop growing, our body starts to die. But it's also true mentally. When it comes to our emotions, our capacities, and our talents, if we aren't growing them, then we're losing them. If we aren't expanding our horizons, then we're allowing them to close in on us. If we aren't demanding more from our lives and from ourselves, then we're settling for less.

Expect the discomfort of change and learn to embrace it as proof that you're still alive, still vigorous, still growing. The moment you stop changing, you stop growing. The moment you stop growing, you stop living.

Cultivate change; accept discomfort; insist on growth. When you do, your comfort zone will expand to make your wishes come true.

8

Time

You have your wish, you have your plan, and you're taking the actions necessary to make your wish come true. Now all you have to do is to give it time.

There are two kinds of time. The first kind is measured by the number of hours you are willing to devote to a task during a single day. I call this *vertical time*. The second kind is measured by the number of days you are willing to devote to a task in order to complete it. I call this *horizontal time*. The maximum *vertical time* at our command is 24 hours because that's all the time there is in a day. The maximum *horizontal time* at our command is an entire lifetime. Which kind of time do you think is more powerful?

All hours are not created equal. If there were a crack in a dam behind your house and it took 24 hours to fix it, you wouldn't work on it an hour a day for 24 days, would you? You would work on it around the clock, before the dam burst and washed your house away. What if you wanted to grow some flowers in a garden in front of that same house? You wouldn't work on it 24 hours a day, would you? You and the flowers would be better off if you gave them an hours worth of attention every day for 24 days.

Some tasks require vertical time. Others require horizontal time. Choosing the right kind of time for the job is half the battle. Most people approach their problems as if they were repairing a dam that is about to break. But most problems are more like tending a garden than they are like fixing a dam. Most of what you want to accomplish in life you can accomplish better, and with greater enjoyment, if you do it over time, instead of trying to do it all at once.

Unfortunately, the frantic pace of life points us in the opposite direction. Haste has become an end in itself. We would rather work feverishly on a project for a few days, than work steadily for a few weeks. We would rather get rich quickly than get rich slowly. And that's where we miss the boat.

It's a lot harder to get rich quickly than it is to get rich slowly. It's a lot harder to accomplish anything of value in a few days than it is to accomplish the same thing in a few months. When you try to cram too much into a single day, or a few days, time is working against you. But when you spread your efforts over time, time is on your side.

Devote even a few minutes a day to a project, and with enough days, you can accomplish almost anything. If you work on your wish over time, over time your wish will come true.

Given enough horizontal time, you can learn to play a musical instrument, master a foreign language, read the collected works of William Shakespeare, dig yourself a swimming pool, earn a college degree, build an addition on your house, learn a trade, write a book, land a new job, start a company, or all of the above. It might take you a year, or it might take you twenty years; so what?

Don't get hung up on how long it will take; that's just another way to derail your dreams. Think of the middle-aged woman who wanted to go to law school but was afraid she was too old. "It will take me three years to finish," she explained to a friend, "and by then I'll be fifty-seven." Her friend asked, "How old will you be in three years if you don't go to law school?"

Who cares how old you are? Who cares how long your LAMP Plan will take? The time will pass anyway; why not put it to good use?

The gift of hindsight

When I was a senior in college, I decided that I was going to become a writer. But for the next dozen years I barely wrote a thing. One afternoon while I was sitting at my desk daydreaming, I had one of those life-changing revelations that comes out of nowhere and takes a baseball bat to the side of your head:

If you had decided to write a couple of sentences a day twelve years ago, by now you would have completed half-a-dozen books.

I was stunned. In a single pathetic moment I realized just how much time I had wasted, and how easily I could have prevented it. It was as if twelve years of my life had just floated by without me, while I stood on the shore and watched. All because I didn't have the brains to write a couple of sentences a day. What kind of a fool was I?

Before I could answer that, a new thought presented itself, shining like a sunbeam punching it's way through a thundercloud:

You're missing the point—this is a wake-up call, not Judgment Day.

I finally got it. I finally understood what the world was trying to beat into my head. The point of life is not to grieve over what you wasted in the past, but to make certain that you don't waste the future. I had been shown failure so that I could learn from it and turn it into success. All I had to do was to write a couple of sentences a day *from that point on*, and my dreams of being a writer would come true.

Hallelujah! I had been handed one of the secrets of the universe. I was delighted, elated, and overjoyed. I was also terrified.

What if I couldn't change? What if I couldn't muster even the minimal effort necessary to write a sentence or two a day? I'd never been able to do it before; what made me I think I could do it now?

As if on cue, my thoughts leaped twelve years into the future. There I could see myself wringing my hands in frustration because I still hadn't written a thing. I was miserable, a wretched failure, accused and tormented by regret. I knew I would remain a failure until my dying day. I knew I would live without joy, without reward, without happiness, without …

That did it. I'd had enough. I was a changed man. As surely as I knew my own name, I knew I would never let that kind of future take place. Like Scrooge on Christmas morning, I had seen the Ghost of Things Yet To Come, and he had scared the daylights out of me. I had been given a second chance, and I would make the most of it. The next twelve years would see a very different me from the twelve years just passed.

We are all wise in hindsight. The secret to making your wishes come true is to turn hindsight into foresight. Use your past to empower your future. Begin today what you regret not having done yesterday, and you will avoid that regret tomorrow.

Ellis's Law

Once I began to write every day, the results astonished me. Even when I managed no more than a sentence or two, over time my sentences formed paragraphs, the paragraphs formed chapters, and the chapters formed books—like magic.

But it wasn't magic; it was a simple principle that lies behind all human accomplishment: *Even ordinary effort over time yields extraordinary results.* I call this *Ellis's Law*, not because I'm the first one to discover it, but because when it discovered me, it changed my life. It's the heart and soul of how I've made my wishes come true. It's the magic behind my magic lamp.

Even ordinary effort over time yields extraordinary results. This is the single most important idea in *The Magic Lamp*, the single most useful piece of advice I can give you to help you make your wishes come true. If you take it to heart, if you act on it—even if you ignore everything else you find in these pages—you'll multiply a hundredfold your chances for success. You'll enlist in your cause the most irresistible force in the universe: *time.*

We're surrounded by testimony to the power of time. The gentle hills on the horizon were once great mountains; the great mountains were once the ocean floor. That sapling we planted years ago grows too slowly for us to notice, yet now it shades the whole house. A bricklayer places a single brick at a time, yet before we know it, he builds a skyscraper. A small drip from a faucet soon fills a bathtub, and given enough time would fill an ocean. We buy a CD of our favorite music, add another and then another over the years, and before we know it our music collection is worth more than our car. We munch an extra cookie after dinner once or twice a week, and the next time we step on the scale, we've gained twenty pounds. Whatever we do over time, we magnify by the time over which we do it. It's as if we collect compound interest on everything we do, whenever we do it long enough.

When I refer to "ordinary effort," I don't mean to suggest that your efforts should be ordinary. Extraordinary effort over time produces even better results. But most of us already know this. We've heard the stories of successful people who have worked extraordinarily hard and produced spectacular results. What most of us miss is the notion that *any* effort can produce results—astonishing results—if we give it enough time.

We don't have to work sixteen hours a day to write a book; we can work twenty minutes a day over the next few years. We don't have to earn a million dollars in the next year to become a millionaire; we can save a few dollars a week for twenty years and accomplish the same thing. We don't have to lose fifty pounds during the next month to look good; we can lose a pound a week for the next fifty weeks and come out looking just as good. We don't have to get that college degree all at once (or build that rec room, or learn that new language, or earn that promotion); we can work on it an hour or two a day for as long as it takes.

Find the time to succeed

Success takes time, even if it's just a few minutes a day. You may feel you don't have a lot of time. You may feel rushed, perhaps even crushed by the pace of life. You may be asking yourself: *How will I ever find the time to work a wish into a schedule like mine?*

That's the wrong question to ask. Instead of starting with your schedule and trying to work in your wish, start with your wish and then try to work in the rest of your schedule. If you're going to shortchange something, short-change the things that are at the bottom of your list of priorities, not the things at the top. Make this one change in how you spend your day—work on what is most important to you *before* you take care of everything else—and you'll find that your schedule begins to take on the shape of a life, instead of your life taking on the shape of a schedule.

That still leaves the question: Where will you find the time to get it all done? Many of us don't have to look far. A recent study by Nielsen Media Research found that 98 percent of the homes in the United States have television sets. The average man watches 3 hours and 44 minutes of television every day. The average woman watches 4 hours and 25 minutes. The average teenager watches an average of 2 hours and 43 minutes a day. If you watch as much TV as the average American—even if you watch only half as much—you can find all the time you need to make your wish come true just by turning a portion of your TV-time into wish-time. Whether it's an hour a day, or half an hour a day, or even 15 minutes a day, every minute helps. Every minute you spend in front of your wish instead of in front of your TV will move you one minute closer to making your wish come true.

Am I suggesting that you have to give up television to make your wishes come true? Of course not. You probably don't watch as much TV as the average American anyway, or you wouldn't have found the time to read this book. Watch as much TV as you like. Just keep this in mind: Of the TV you do watch, there isn't a moment that gets you closer to making your wishes come true. If you want more out of life than you're getting now, you have to transform time that isn't giving you what you want into time that is giving you what you want.

It's not a matter of giving up TV or giving up anything else you like to do. It's a matter of doing what is most important to you *first*. For example, suppose one evening you were about to settle down in front of your favorite TV program when a little voice asked, "Which is more important to you: to make your wish come true or to watch this show?" Which would you choose? Choose your wish, and you're on your way to making that wish come true. Choose your TV program, and you're on your way to watching it. Your wish will just have to wait until it becomes more important than your show. It's as simple as that.

TV-time isn't the only time you can use to work on your wish. Do you read the newspaper each morning? It's great to be informed, but is that more important to you than making your wishes come true? Do you read dime-store novels to escape from the rat race? If you invest some of your reading time in making your wishes come true, you might not have as much need to escape.

How much time do you spend each morning getting ready for work? Try cutting it by 10 minutes. Then invest those ten minutes in helping to make your wish come true. You would be amazed how much you can accomplish in 10 minutes a day, if you do it every day.

How much time do you spend each day doing chores around the house? Trim a few minutes from each task and use those minutes to work on your wish. You'll still get your chores done, believe it or not, and you'll get your wish done, too.

The time tithe

There are two ways to find enough time to work on your wish. The simplest and most direct way is to schedule the time and then stick to your schedule. I schedule time to work on my wish every morning, first thing, because my wish is the most important thing I have to do each day. You might choose to work on your wish at the end of the day, or in the middle. It doesn't matter when you do it; it matters only that you do it, and do it every day.

The second way to make room each day for your wish is to tithe your time. Simply trim by 10% the time you spend on each of your daily activities. Then invest that extra time in making your wish come true.

You might think you can't possibly trim any time from your daily activities, but you can. The most curious principle of time management is that the less time we have to do something, the more likely we are to get it done. That's why deadlines work. That's why more Americans file their tax returns a week before they're due than file them a month before they're due. That's why stores on Christmas Eve are so full of people doing last-minute shopping—because it's the last minute they can shop.

The second most curious principle of time management is that the less time we have, the more we tend to get done. We force ourselves to set priorities and to focus on them. We force ourselves to concentrate on the things that are most important to us and ignore the rest. That's why we so often accomplish more the day before we leave on vacation than we do the whole week before. The less you have of any precious resource, the more you tend to stretch it to make do.

Start your *time tithe* with your daily routine. For example, you don't have to give up the morning paper; just trim 10% from the time you spend reading it. Trim 10% from the time you spend taking a shower, getting dressed, commuting to work, and then watching TV when you come home. Trim 10% from the time you spend sleeping. Whatever activities you perform each day, give yourself 10% less time to perform each one. This will free two-and-a-half hours every day to devote to your wish, more than enough time to make almost any wish come true.

Work

How can you cut 10% from the time you spend at work? If normally you work more than eight hours a day, you can probably cut back to eight hours without coming to grief with your employer. This will become easier when the two of you realize that the quality of your work will tend to improve the less overtime you give it because you'll be forcing yourself to set priorities and focus your efforts. You will also feel fresher and more energized while you're at work because you'll be spending less time on the job and more time recharging yourself for the next day's work.

But what if you're already working only eight hours a day and your employer refuses to let you trim that by 10%? Just give yourself a work-wish, something that you would very much like to make happen at work. Treat this work-wish like any other wish. Take it through the LAMP Process. Work on it every day. To find time to work on it, trim 10% from the time you spend on each of the other tasks you have to perform during the work day. Ten percent of an eight-hour day is 48 minutes. That's nearly an hour a day you can use to make your work-wish come true.

Sleep

Assuming you average eight hours of sleep a night, if you reduce that by 10% you can reclaim nearly an hour a day to work on your wish. But is it wise to cut into your sleep?

I can't give you medical advice (you should consult your doctor before you decide to change your sleeping habits), but I can tell you what happened to me when I changed my sleeping habits.

A while back I bought a curious little book about how to sleep less and enjoy it more.* The book made two points that really hit home. First, it suggested that the amount of sleep we need seems to be more a matter of habit than of physical necessity. The human body does not require eight hours of sleep each night. There are many people—entire cultures, for that matter—who get by with only six or seven hours of sleep a night. The second point the book made is that someone who is sleeping eight hours every night is probably getting more sleep than he or she needs. Too much sleep can make you as groggy as too little.

I was intrigued with the notion that the eight hours of sleep I thought I required each night might be more of a habit than a necessity. I was equally intrigued by the possibility that I might be able to reduce my sleep by an hour every night and thereby create an extra hour every day to make my wishes come true. With so much at stake, I decided to use my habit-changing tools (visualization, affirmation, pre-memory, and repetition) to form a new habit of sleeping only seven hours a night instead of eight.

For the first few days I felt groggy, but before long I found that seven hours of sleep per night was all I needed. I had more energy during the day than ever before, and I slept better at night. To top it off, I gave myself an extra hour every day to work on my wishes. That was the equivalent of nine extra work weeks every year.

Try the *time tithe* for a month and see what happens.

---

* For the title, see *Resources* at the end of this book.

Trim just 10% from the time you spend on each of your daily activities, then rechannel that 10% toward making your wishes come true. You will be investing your most precious asset—your time—toward your most important objective—your wish. Elementary as this may sound, it's the most important thing you can do to make your wish come true.

Give yourself time

If your wish is going to take awhile, give it awhile. Give it twice awhile. Make sure your LAMP Plan allows you enough time to make the plan work. Often, when people don't complete a wish in the time they've allowed, they give up and feel like failures. But they aren't failures; they just haven't allowed themselves enough time to get the job done. To make a wish come true, sometimes you have to stick by the wish's schedule instead of your own. You have to give it as much time as it requires. A second less won't do.

The surest way to starve yourself of time is to starve yourself of money. I started a business once that I was certain was going to make me rich. I never worked so hard in my life—sixteen hours a day, seven days a week. I didn't have any money coming in, so I used my savings to pay the bills. When I exhausted my savings, I began to borrow on my credit cards. When I filled my credit cards I began to borrow from my family. Before I knew it I was a mile deep in debt and not an inch closer to success. When I couldn't beg or borrow any more money, I closed my business and went to work for someone else.

The business wasn't a bad idea, but the business plan was. It didn't provide enough money to complete the plan. I should have kept my day job and developed my business part-time. Then I would have had all the income I needed to keep the doors open long enough for my business to take hold. A day job would have given me the horizontal time I needed to make the business work.

Years later, I found myself in a similar situation. I wanted to become a writer. But I wasn't about to quit my day job to write. I knew better. I knew it would take months to finish the first book I had in mind. Then it would take months to sell it to a publisher, if I sold it at all. Then it would take a year before the book found its way into bookstores, and several more years before I had written and sold enough books even to begin to pay my bills. The only way I could give myself the horizontal time I needed to succeed as a writer was to write part-time, and keep my day job for as long as it would take me to become a success.

So that's what I did. It took years. It took years longer than I had imagined. But it worked, because this time around I didn't starve my wish. I never ran out of cash, so I never ran out of time. I allowed myself as much time as I needed to make my wish come true, so it came true.

If you find yourself tempted to quit your day job to pursue your wish, go ahead, as long as you have enough money in the bank to keep yourself going for *twice* as long as you think it will take. If you don't have that much money socked away, do yourself and your wish a favor—keep your day job. If you don't have a day job, get one that pays the bills. Don't think of it as giving up on your wish; think of it as funding your wish so you don't have to give up on it. Your day job can give you all the resources you need to work on your wish for as long as it takes to make that wish come true.

Spare-time wishing may not feel like the ideal arrangement. It may not get you where you want to go as fast as you want to get there, but it will get you there faster than going broke. And it really works. As a young man, Albert Einstein worked as a patent clerk. In his spare time, he invented the Theory of Relativity. Anything is possible if you give it enough time.

Take your time

Once you've given yourself enough time to make your wish come true, take the time. I feel the most stressed and the least productive when I rush through a task. But when I allow myself to take my time, I relax and the quality of my work improves. I feel more creative and more energetic, and I get more done.

Better yet, I enjoy it more. I enjoy almost any task as long as I'm not racing through it to get to the next one. Even chores like washing dishes and mowing the lawn lose their sense of drudgery when I allow myself to take my time.

In taking my time, I give myself permission to enjoy what I'm doing. This works even when I'm facing a deadline. Whenever I find myself focusing more on the deadline than on what I'm doing, I change the deadline to give myself some breathing room. Once I'm free to take my time, I'm free to enjoy my time, and I'm that much more likely to do my best work.

Take your time, and you'll find that you begin to enjoy what you're doing. Enjoy what you're doing, and you'll find that before you know it you've completed everything necessary to make your wish come true.

9

Problems

Problems are a sign of life. The only human beings without problems are buried six feet underground. So don't wish for fewer problems, wish for more skill in solving them.

Problems exist because there are far more ways for things to go wrong than for things to go right. You can misspell a word a hundred ways, but there is just one way to spell it right. You can give a thousand wrong answers to a math problem, but there is just one right answer. There are more ways to clutter your house than to keep it clean. There are more ways to lose a sale than to make one.

Making your wishes come true is a matter of solving whatever problems stand in your way. At birth, you were given the most powerful problem-solving computer in the world: a human brain. The trick to solving any problem is to persuade that brain to do what it does best—*think*.

What follows is a three-step thinking process that will help you solve any problem you encounter.

Step 1:   *Decide what problem you want to solve.*

Suppose you wake up Monday morning after a two-week vacation, start to get dressed, and discover you've gained so much weight that none of your clothes fit. Which of these is the real problem:

A)   Your body is too big.
B)   Your clothes are too small.
C)   You don't have anything to wear to work.

The answer: They are all real problems. You can't even begin to think about a solution until you decide which of these problems you want to solve. If you decide to solve all three of them, you have to decide which one you're going to solve first.

Step 2:   *Choose the solution.*

There is more than one way to solve a problem. For example, if you don't have anything to wear to work, you can race out and buy some new clothes. Or you can borrow some clothes. Or you can make some clothes. Or you can quit.

The solution you choose to any problem depends on the result you want to produce. For instance, if you find yourself in an unhappy marriage, you have to decide whether you want to save your marriage or get out of it. If you have a dead-end job, you have to decide whether you want a promotion, or a transfer, or a new employer. If your car breaks down, you have to decide whether you want to fix it or buy another car. Once you choose the result you want, you enable yourself to choose a course of action that will cause that result to happen.

Brainstorming session

You can come up with a whole range of solutions for even your toughest problems if you think of a solution as nothing more than an answer to an appropriate question. Just ask yourself the question and listen to your answers. Sound familiar? It should. It's nothing but brainstorming, and you already know how to do that. Here's how you can use the five steps of brainstorming to help you solve any problem you encounter:

Step 1: *Write the problem you want to solve, in the form of a question, at the top of a clean sheet of paper.*

To tap the problem-solving power of your own mind, you have only to ask it a question and then listen to your answers.

Step 2: *Write whatever pops into your head.*

Ask yourself the question you've written at the top of your page, then write every answer that springs to mind.

Step 3: *Accept with gratitude whatever pops into your head.*

Your brain is a gold mine, or as I like to think of it, a *gold mind*. Mine it for all it's worth. Accept every thought as if it were a nugget of pure gold.

Trust yourself. Your most bizarre ideas may, in the light of day, prove to be your best. Or your best ideas may be lurking just behind an outrageous thought, and you have to drag that outrageous thought out of your mind, and out of the way, before you can get to the real gold.

Step 4:　Keep your pen moving.

Tell yourself you're going to brainstorm for two minutes, or five, or whatever. Then keep your pen moving until the time is up.

Step 5:　Save your criticism for later

Write, don't judge. You'll have plenty of time later to judge.

When you have completed your brainstorming session, you will have a list of possible solutions to the problem you wrote at the top of your paper. You can then decide which solutions you want to pursue and file the rest.

The more you practice brainstorming, the better you'll become. Before you know it, you'll be able to reel off bankable solutions as easily as you can recite the days of the week.

Look for at least two solutions

There are at least two solutions for any problem, and probably a great many more. Once you find one solution, keep looking for another, and then another. Keep your mind open. Instead of telling yourself to look for that one perfect solution, tell yourself to look for the best solution among alternatives. Then keep looking for alternatives. Keep asking yourself questions. Keep listening to your answers. As long as you do, your mind will continue to serve them to you on a silver platter.

Approach the problem from a fresh perspective.

Would you describe the shape below as convex or concave?

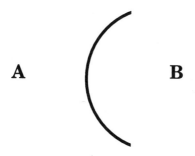

Your answer depends on your perspective. If you're looking at it from the right side, where the "B" is, it looks concave. If you're looking at it from the left side, where the "A" is, it looks convex. Simply by shifting your point of view, you can change one description of "reality" into its exact opposite.

Next time you face a tough problem, try looking at it from a fresh perspective. The problem will take on a whole new meaning and present you with a range of new solutions.

For example, lumber mills used to have an awful time

disposing of sawdust. It was inconvenient and expensive. It was also a fact of life for the lumber business, until someone came along and looked at the problem from a fresh perspective. Instead of seeing waste, this man saw raw material. Instead of seeing sawdust, he saw Presto Logs. By adding a little wax to the sawdust and a fancy wrapper, he created a new product that made him rich and allowed lumber mills to make money selling sawdust, instead of paying to have it hauled away.

In every "unsolvable" problem is the seed of a solution. To recognize that solution, all you have to do is to look at the problem in a new light. Come at each of your problems from a fresh perspective, and you will be able to create no end of fresh solutions.

Look For The Obvious

Legend has it that one rush hour, a tractor-trailer got stuck in the Holland Tunnel in New York City. The truck was too tall to move forward and wedged too tightly to move backward. The police, already on the scene, called in the fire department. They drew all their best minds together to consider the problem and came up with what seemed like the only logical solution: saw off the top of the tractor-trailer and tow the rig out of the tunnel.

Then a car drove by in the opposite lane. Inside, a little girl asked her dad why didn't they just let the air out of the truck's tires? Her dad pulled over and asked the police. They scratched their heads, looked embarrassed, and followed the little girl's advice. Within minutes, they had the truck clear of the tunnel.

The little girl was too young and too naive to look for difficult solutions, so she came up with an easy one. Keep that in mind next time you face a tough problem. Look for solutions right under your nose, where they're so obvious you might be inclined to ignore them, like a pair of slacks you can't find in the closet because they're hanging in front of your eyes.

What if?

What if the next time you hear yourself say, *That will never work,* you quickly add, *But what if I try it anyway?*

When you ask *What if?* you allow yourself to consider all your options, to try them on for size, without risk. You open yourself to possibilities that would otherwise remain hidden from you. You allow yourself to explore all the potential solutions to a problem, instead of just the ones that seem politically correct. Armed with more choices, you improve your chances of making the right one.

Give yourself advice

Another great way to come up with creative solutions is to ask yourself this:

> *If I happened upon someone with the same problem I am trying to solve, what advice would I give to that person?*

For example, suppose you would like to change careers. You want to start over in a new field that interests you, instead of spending the rest of your life in the same mind-numbing business you stumbled into when you finished school. But you have a family to support, bills to pay, a mortgage check to write every month. How can you make the switch from one career to another without giving up your standard of living?

To answer this question, pretend you're riding in an airplane and you strike up a conversation with the person sitting beside you. He tells you he's dying to change careers, but he can't afford to give up his standard of living. What advice would you give him?

Would you tell him to make the change, or else in ten years he'll find himself exactly where he is now? Would you tell him he will perform so much better in a job he loves than in a job he hates, that he will actually raise his standard of living? Would you tell him that finding fulfillment and happiness in life is more important than buying a new car every three years? Would you tell him that life is too short to waste in the wrong career? Sure you would! You would tell him all these things because it's easier to give advice than it is to follow it.

Following good advice is hard work—too hard for most of us, so all too often we tend to hide our best advice from ourselves. To get the benefit of our own best advice, sometimes we have to pretend we're giving that advice to someone else.

Don't even think about it

I call my wife so often at her work that I dial her number without thinking. But if you asked me her number—if you asked me to think about it—I would have to dial it to answer your question.

Remember when you learned how to drive a car? First you had to learn the rules of the road—right of way, speed limits, safe-driving tips. Then you had to learn how to operate your vehicle. You had to master the steering wheel, the transmission, the gas pedal, the brakes. Then, probably in a parking lot, you had to practice using all of these unfamiliar controls in unison, preferably without driving the car through the side of a building. Finally, you had to put it all together on a real highway and somehow maneuver a 3,000 pound projectile from *Point A* to *Point B*, while hundreds of other projectiles raced by you at 60 miles an hour. All without killing yourself or your poor driving instructor. All while keeping in mind everything you had just learned about safe driving.

Of course, you couldn't keep it all in mind, at least not consciously. You weren't any good at driving until you learned to drive unconsciously. The better your driving, the more unconscious your driving skills became. Within weeks, not only were you able to cruise comfortably at the speed limit, but far beyond it—with a Coke in one hand, a hamburger in the other, and your free arm around your date, all the while chatting happily with the couple in the back seat.

There is more about you than meets the eye. The most powerful part of your mind, the part responsible for your skills, your emotions, your memory, and your deepest thinking, is subconscious. Most of you is below the surface. You might not know it's there, and you might not know what it's doing, but it's running the show—your show. Your subconscious mind is the single most powerful tool you can command to solve problems. To unleash this power, you have only to learn how to let your subconscious do your thinking for you.

Have you ever taken a test where you knew an answer, but you couldn't remember it while you were sitting in the classroom? Then the bell rang, you walked out the door, and the answer popped into your head. Your subconscious finally got around to giving you the answer once you let go of the question. Therein lies the secret to tapping the power of the subconscious. Let go of the question with your conscious mind, and your subconscious mind will provide the answer.

Your best thinking is done subconsciously. That's why we get so many of our best ideas at the strangest times—in the shower, just before we drop off to sleep, driving to work, wolfing down a steak sub—while our conscious mind is preoccupied with other things.

To put your subconscious mind to work solving problems, follow these three steps:

1. *Turn your problem into a question, and then ask yourself the question.*

   For example, if the problem you are trying to solve is that you can't stop falling asleep at work, you might ask yourself, *How can I stay alert and energized all day long?*

2. *Once you have asked yourself the question, let go of it and turn your attention to something else.*

   Your answer may not come for hours, or even days. But don't worry, it will come. If you *do* worry, it may not come. It may hover in the wings, like an actor afraid to appear on stage, until you turn your attention somewhere else.

   If you don't come up with an answer within two or three days, ask yourself the question again, and then let go of it again. Repeat this cycle for as long as it takes to get your question answered. Trust your subconscious. Expect answers. They will come.

3. *Write your answers the moment they come to you.*

   Ideas are like lottery tickets you can print for

yourself. You just keep printing them until you win. But you can't cash them in unless you write them down.

When you commit your thoughts to paper, you let your subconscious know you're listening, so it's more inclined to give you something to listen to. If you ignore what it gives you, it will stop giving it to you.

When you commit your thoughts to paper the moment they occur, you capture ideas that would otherwise vanish again into your subconscious, like a fish slips off a hook and disappears into the sea. If you think an idea will hang around for a day, or an hour, or even a few minutes, until you find the time to write it down, you're fooling yourself, and you're throwing away your most valuable resource. The weakest ink is mightier than the most powerful memory. Whatever you write down, you cannot forget. If you put your thoughts in writing before they leave you, they will never leave you.

I keep a pad of paper and a pen everywhere I go—in my car, my bathroom, my briefcase, beside my bed, in my pocket—just in case I get an idea. I don't want to lose even a single idea because I lacked the good sense to write it down. Nothing is more powerful than an idea whose time has come; nothing is more useless than an idea whose time has come and gone because it was forgotten. An idea is a terrible thing to waste—*write it down.*

There is no better time to ask yourself a problem-solving question than just before you fall asleep because we do some of our best thinking while we sleep. That's why when we face a tough decision so often we decide to "sleep on it".

When you ask yourself a question at bedtime, let go of it. Let the answer come in its own good time. Enjoy your sleep in the relaxed assurance that the answer will be waiting for you in the morning. If you think about your question consciously, you will only keep yourself awake. But if you sleep on it, you will let your subconscious do the work while you rest the night away.

Like anything else you want to master, the process of tapping your subconscious mind will take some practice, but the practice is easy. All you have to do is to ask yourself a question and record the answers when they come. The more you exercise your problem-solving muscles, the stronger they become, and the better able to solve the problems that stand between you and making your wish come true.

Step 3:   *Take action to solve the problem.*

When it comes to facing a problem, there are two types of people in the world: those who ask, *Why me?* and those who ask, *What am I going to do about it?* In this single question lies the difference between the great and the ingrate, the champion and the chump, the winner and the whiner.

Any idiot can tell you what's wrong with the world. The movers and shakers do something about it. The best solution in the world won't solve a problem unless you take the action necessary to put that solution to work. Act, and you will solve the problem. Don't act, and you will become the problem.

10

Help

You alone are responsible for making your wishes come true. You alone are the one who has to make things happen. You alone make or break your own success. But your greatest resource is other people.

Whatever effort you can make on your own, you can multiply by enlisting the help of other people. Other people have resources you don't have: a different point of view, different ideas, different skills, different experiences, different contacts, a different checking account. When you enlist other people in your cause, their resources become your resources.

The people you already know can help you ask for help from literally anyone in the country. For example, suppose you're a high-school student and you want to ask a favor of the President of the United States. First, you would talk to someone you already know—a teacher, your school principal, a coach, or perhaps the owner of the business where you work during summer vacation. Let's assume that you've decided to approach the business owner. Chances are that he or she knows many of the leading citizens of your community. One of these leading citizens most likely knows the congressman from your area. You can be sure that your congressman has the clout to place a phone call to the President of the United States.

Your plan of action would be to ask the business owner, to ask the community leader, to ask the congressman, to ask the President for a favor on your behalf. Four steps, and you're at the very top. If you can reach the President this easily, you can reach anyone else you care to reach.

Think of someone who might help you make your wish come true. If you've written a book, you might want to contact a publisher. If you're trying to land your dream job, you might want to reach the person who is hiring. If you're trying to get your big break as an actor, you might want to reach a Hollywood producer. If you want to become a roadie for your favorite rock-and-roll band, you might want to reach the band's manager. If you're trying to get into graduate school, you might want to reach the director of admissions. Think of anyone in the country (or the world, for that matter), and then think of how you might reach that person through the people you already know.

For instance, suppose you want to have your resume considered by the one person in the world who can hire you for your dream job. Lets say this person happens to be a vice president of the CBS Television Network. Think of someone you know who works for CBS. If you don't know anyone, think of someone you know who might know someone who works for CBS (at the local CBS television station, for example). Once you make contact with someone who works for CBS, you'll find that he or she knows somebody (a boss, or a boss's boss, perhaps) who knows somebody (an executive) who knows the vice president you're trying to reach. It's that simple. In fact, the more successful the person you want to reach, the more people he or she knows, so the easier it is to reach that person through other people.

People can help you in so many ways. They can give you advice, training, money, feedback, contacts, and emotional support. They can make the difference between spectacular success and lonely failure. They can give you everything you need to make your wish come true. There's just one catch: if you want their help you're going to have to ask for it. When you do, you might as well stack the deck in your favor. Below is a five-step strategy that will help you earn a *Yes* when you ask for something, instead of a *No*.

1.   *Ask for something specific.*

The best way to help someone help you is to be specific about what you're asking for. If your helper doesn't know exactly what you want, how can he or she help you get it? For that matter, if you don't know exactly what you want, how can you ask for it?

Help your helper help you. If you force him to fill in the blanks, he'll probably fill them in wrong. Or he might not help you at all because he doesn't understand what you want. If you don't understand, how can he?

Be specific. If you're asking for money, ask for exactly the amount you need and when you need it. If you're asking for an introduction to someone, specify who, and when, and exactly what you want your helper to say on your behalf. If you're asking for advice, ask your advisor for a specific solution to a specific problem. If you're asking for emotional support, ask for precisely the kind of support you need. If you aren't specific in what you ask for, you won't get it.

2.   *Ask someone who can help you get it.*

Before you ask for something, first ask this question of yourself: *Can this person give me what I'm asking for?* If the answer is *No*, then find someone who can.

If you want money, ask someone who can give it to you or can help you get it. If you want a promotion or a new job, ask someone who can promote you, or hire you, or put you in touch with someone who can. If you want to sell something, ask someone who has the power to buy it. If you want to buy something, ask someone who has the power to sell it. When you go to the trouble to ask for something, make sure you ask someone who can give it to you.

Nowhere is this more important—and more misunderstood—than when it comes to asking for advice. Our first tendency is to ask for advice from the people we know best. Too often, they are more than willing to help but are less than helpful.

For example, we ask our parents how to become wealthy, although they have never become wealthy themselves. We ask our best friend how to get a promotion, although he can't hold a job. We ask our neighbor how to lose weight, although she can no longer fit into the dress she bought last week. They all mean well; they just don't know well. They don't know enough about the task at hand to be of help.

Unless someone has already been where you want to go, the chances are that he or she can't tell you how to get there. If you want good advice, ask someone who has already achieved what you want to achieve and can tell you from experience how you can do the same. Ask someone who can help.

3. *Make it worthwhile for the person you ask.*

People may help you out of love; they may help you out of compassion; but they will definitely help you out of self-interest. If you want someone to help you, make it worth his while.

When you ask for something, the question that is most likely to form in the mind of the person you're asking is this: *What's in it for me?* How you answer that question will largely determine whether or not that person is willing to help you.

You have to do more than make a reasonable request. You have to make your request so attractive that the other person feels it's unreasonable to deny it. If you can find a way to sufficiently enrich his life, he will eagerly enrich yours. If you can find a way to serve him, you will be amazed how willingly he serves you. You don't have to convince him, you don't have to persuade him, you don't have to pressure him. You have only to make it worth his while. The rest will take care of itself.

4. *Be sincere*

I don't mean *act* sincere; I mean *be* sincere. It's not a matter of how you come across; it's a matter of how you feel. Do you really want what you're asking for? If not, how can you expect someone else to want to give it to you? Are you certain about what you want? If not, the person you're asking for help will be uncertain about giving it to you.

Whenever you feel a conflict on the inside, it shows on

the outside. It makes people more likely to resist you than to help you. If you have doubts about what you want, convince yourself first, before you try to convince anyone else. Then, when you're sure about what you want, you can ask for it sincerely, with absolute conviction. The more convinced you are about what you want, the more likely you are to convince someone else to help you get it.

5. *Keep asking until you get what you want.*

Some people hear the word *No* and give up. Other people hear *No* and think that all they need is a bigger hammer. When they find one, they keep pounding until they hear a *Yes*. I don't recommend either approach.

No means that what you're doing isn't working, so try something else. You don't need a hammer; you need a key— a key that will unlock the other person's heart.

Maybe you haven't asked the right question yet. Maybe you haven't made it worth that person's while. Maybe you haven't been specific enough. Maybe you haven't been sincere. Somewhere along the line you haven't done whatever it is you need to do to inspire that person to help you. So try something else. Or try someone else. And keep trying until you get what you want. If you keep trying until you get what you ask for, you will always get what you ask for.

LA<u>M</u>P Process

Step Three:

<u>M</u>anage Your Results

11

Focus

When you were a child did you ever use a magnifying glass to burn your initials into a block of wood? What was it about that glass that turned the gentle warmth of the sun into a powerful heat-ray?

In a word, *focus*. Focus means to converge upon a single point. Focused energy can accomplish what that same energy, when dispersed, cannot.

Most people are like the sun on a warm day; they radiate their energy broadly, with no particular object in mind. In living out one day, they accomplish little beyond making it to the next.

Successful people are like a magnifying glass. They focus their energy—and their time and their talent—on exactly what they want to achieve. They know that their power is greatest when it's focused to a single point. They are no better than other people; they are no smarter; they are no more worthy. They possess no more time, or energy, or talent. But they are more focused. They use focus to accomplish what seems beyond their power.

If you want to have the broadest effect on your life, focus on the narrowest point. Concentrate your time, your energy, and your talent on making happen the one thing you most want to happen.

Military strategists call this *concentration of force*. They know that the way to win a battle is to meet the enemy with everything you've got at a point where your forces will overwhelm his. The same tactic can help you make your wish come true. Think of "the enemy" as whatever obstacle stands between you and the completion of your wish. Then focus all your effort on overwhelming that obstacle.

Focus means you put your wish first, ahead of all the other things that compete for your attention. You make time every day for your wish—half an hour, an hour, two hours, whatever you're willing to set aside—before you make time for everything else. It's not that you have to give up everything else, you simply refuse to let everything else make you give up your wish. That's focus.

Keep your wish in front of you.

To keep your efforts focused on your wish, keep your wish in front of you. Some people like to post their wish where they'll see it every day—on their bathroom mirror, on the dashboard of their car, atop their computer screen. Others prefer to write their wish on a card and keep the card in their wallet. Whenever they have a free moment during the day—waiting for the subway, holding on the phone, standing in line at the checkout counter—they can pull out the card and read their wish.

One thing that works especially well is to write your wish every day instead of reading it. Writing it over and over burns it into your mind and gives you ample incentive to strip away every unnecessary word. The shorter the wish, the greater the emotional impact.

Affirm your wish

The most effective way I've found to keep myself focused on the wish at hand is to repeat it every day, just like an affirmation. I repeat it aloud, with intense emotion, until I feel it sink in. The number of repetitions isn't nearly as important as the intensity of the emotion.

I say my wish-affirmation at the same time and in the same place every day—in my car on the way to the office. By doing so, I've made it a habit. Each morning when I slide behind the wheel, the first thing I think about is my wish. I find myself repeating it automatically. It gets my morning off to a great start because I know I will spend the entire day focused on making my wish come true.

Another way I keep my wish in front of me is to make a weekly progress report. These reports are built into my LAMP Plan, and scheduled in my weekly calendar. I record how much progress I've made during the past week and compare it to what I expected to make. This keeps me focused on my milestones and deadlines, and lets me make adjustments to my plan before it's too late.

In the rush of your busy schedule, you might be tempted to skip your progress reports. After all, you know how much progress you're making, right? Wrong. If you skip your progress reports, don't be surprised to find yourself a month, or six months, or a year down the road only to realize you're on the wrong road. If you've got that kind of time to waste, by all means skip the reports. But if you want to make every day count, track your progress and stay on top of your LAMP Plan. That will keep you focused like nothing else can.

One wish at a time

If you write your wish every day, affirm it every day, and make a progress report every week, you'll find it exceptionally empowering. If you try to do all of this with several wishes at once, you'll find it exceptionally tedious.

Wishing works because wishing is work. If you pile on too much of that kind of work, you can lose your edge and your enthusiasm. Don't make your life a chore; make it a joy. Work on one wish at a time. Power comes from focus; focus comes from priorities. So set your priorities. Decide what is the most important thing for you to accomplish and work on that until you accomplish it. Once you have completed that wish, you'll be free to work on the next one, and the next one, and then the one after that, until one day you will look back and see behind you a shimmering trail of all the dreams you've made come true.

Refocus

An airliner flying from London to New York is off course 95% of the time. The pilot spends most of the flight making adjustments to put the plane back on course.

That's how you can expect to spend most of your time, too, when you're in the process of making a wish come true. Conditions will change, your LAMP Plan will change, your wish itself may change, and you will confront every imaginable distraction. With all this going on, you will find yourself off course most of the time. Don't beat yourself up about it; just refocus. Make the necessary adjustments. Keep making adjustments—focus, refocus, and refocus again—

until you reach your destination.

That's the secret of being in it for the long haul: you can refocus whenever you need to. Successful people aren't successful because they're always on track; they're successful because they can always get back on track. They know how to refocus, no matter how far off course they might get.

Luck

Like a television set, your mind can tune into what interests you and ignore the rest. There is far more happening around you than you care to pay attention to. You don't notice every knickknack on every desk, every speck of dust on every carpet, every piece of paper in every wastebasket. You don't listen to every snippet of every conversation or every word the announcer is saying on the radio or TV that's playing in the background. You ignore the things that aren't important to you so you can concentrate on the things that are.

Focus is the way you tell your brain what to pay attention to. Once you tune your brain into a particular channel—by focusing on your wish, for example—you begin to notice all sorts of things around you that you didn't know were there.

You begin to notice resources you didn't know you had. Your best friend, it turns out, knows a woman who can get you that job interview you want. Your neighbor owns a cabin in the woods where you can go to write your novel. Rummaging through the attic, you come across your old stamp collection and realize you can sell it to raise the seed money you need to open your part-time business. An old friend calls to ask you to diner and happens to be just the person you need to help you solve a problem that has you stumped.

You begin to notice coincidences. On the airplane sitting beside you is the key contact you've been looking for to help you move your wish along. You thumb through a magazine and find an article that tells you exactly what you need to know to complete the next step in your LAMP Plan. You attend a party and find yourself being introduced to a woman of influence who can help you grant your wish. You're channel surfing through Sunday morning TV and happen across a talk-show interview with a person who has accomplished exactly what you want to accomplish and is explaining how to go about it. The world calls this "luck". I call it focus.

Have you ever envied someone who was lucky enough to be in the right place at the right time? Who knows how often you've been at the right place, at the right time, and didn't recognize it because you lacked focus? When you don't know what you want, you miss all the opportunities that will help you get it. But when you do know what you want, when you're focused, every place is the right place; every time is the right time.

When you focus on your wish, the whole world comes into focus around you. Lucky breaks converge on you like friends converge on a keg party. You invite all the resources at your command, and all those you didn't know you could command, to help you make your wish come true.

12

Connection

A LAMP Plan can take weeks, or months, or even years to complete. That's a long time to stay up for anything. What do you do when you feel tired, or bored, or worst of all, discouraged?

These feelings are a warning to you that you've lost your emotional connection with your wish. You've become unplugged from the source of your power. You're going through the motions, but you're no longer feeling the emotions. You've lost touch with whatever it was that energized you to pursue your wish in the first place.

You can keep pushing yourself and disciplining yourself, but that's not much fun. Why not spare yourself all that pain and hassle and simply reconnect to your wish? Plug yourself back into that wall socket of emotion. Don't force yourself to do what's good for you; inspire yourself.

The secret is to let yourself feel right now the thrill you will eventually feel when you make your wish come true. Enjoy your emotional payoff today instead of waiting until later. Use your emotions to help carry you toward your destination, not just to reward you when you get there. Whatever step you're on—however trivial or tedious it might seem—allow yourself to feel as if you're completing your whole wish.

Enjoy the process. Fall in love with the process the same way you've fallen in love with your wish. Let yourself enjoy every step along the way, no matter how uninspiring any step might be.

For example, if you're training to win the marathon at the Olympics and you're running hundreds of grueling miles every week, you know you're connected to your wish when you feel like every stride in practice is a joy because it's helping you win the Gold.

If you're looking for work and you've already mailed 200 resumes without receiving a single reply, you know you're connected to your wish when you drop yet another resume in the mail and feel great because you've just moved one step closer to success.

If you've recently opened your own company and you've already lost your third order today because your customers think you're inexperienced, you know you're connected to your wish when you can't wait to call that next prospect. Win or lose, you know that every contact you make will take you one step closer to a thriving business.

When you're emotionally connected to your wish, the payoff is *now*. Not tomorrow. Not next year. Right now. You don't have to delay your gratification. You don't have to wait for your reward. With every step you take, you allow yourself to feel the joy of completion, the thrill of success. You keep your eye on the prize and let yourself savor the prize throughout your journey.

When you're connected to your emotional payoff, your LAMP Plan can sail the roughest seas. When you're disconnected, your plan can be swamped by the smallest wave.

Preference questions

Preference questions help you stay connected to your wish. They help you focus your attention and your energy on doing the things today that will help cause your wish to come true tomorrow, even when your natural tendency might be to do just the opposite.

For example, think of your wish as an *ultimate desire* that may from time to time conflict with something you want to do right now—what I call an *immediate desire*. Suppose your ultimate desire is to lose 30 pounds in six months, but your immediate desire is to inhale a hot fudge sundae that is melting in front of your eyes. You know you can put off your ultimate desire, but that hot fudge sundae is right here, right now. You can reach out and touch it, and smell it, and, heaven help you, you can taste it. Chances are you'll be inclined to satisfy your immediate craving at the expense of your ultimate dream. That's called "human nature".

You can try to overcome human nature, through iron-willed self-discipline and denial, but that's the hardest work on earth. Why not work smarter instead of harder? Instead of forcing yourself to toe the line, change the line. Make your ultimate desire and your immediate desire change places. Turn the sundae into something you can put off. Then turn your ideal weight into something you insist on right now.

You can make this all-important switch simply by asking yourself a preference question: *At this instant, would I prefer to be at my ideal weight or have a hot fudge sundae?* Notice that you aren't asking yourself if you would like to reach your ideal weight some time in the future. Instead, you're asking yourself if you would prefer that weight right now, in place of a hot fudge sundae.

Under these circumstances, if you choose the sundae, you might as well give up your wish to lose weight. You have no intention of following through. If you don't prefer your ideal weight to a sundae today, when will you?

But if you choose your ideal weight over a sundae, you're on the right track. You've made an important decision: at this moment, being at your target weight is more important than eating a hot fudge sundae. You've turned an ultimate desire into an immediate desire and given yourself the leverage you need to make your wish come true.

Procrastination

The next step is to turn the hot fudge sundae into something you can put off. You've spent your whole life learning how to procrastinate—why not put it to good use?

Whenever you're tempted to do something now, that will set you back later, put it off. Don't deny it. Don't forbid it. Don't threaten yourself. Just procrastinate. Put off until "tomorrow" whatever might keep you from connecting with your wish today.

The beauty of procrastination is that it gives you nothing to resist. There is nothing to rebel against. Instead of saying *No*, you're saying *Later*. When *Later* comes, the urge may have passed. If not, just put it off again. Keep putting it off, and *Later* will never come. You'll be free to connect to your wish, enjoy your emotional payoff, and turn it into the mental fuel you need to make your wish come true.

13

Flexibility

If what you're doing isn't working, try something else. If you've tried unsuccessfully to smash through a brick wall, go around it. If you can't go around it, go under it. If you can't go under it, go over it. If you can't go over it, then have it moved. Keep trying new options until one of them works. That's the meaning of flexibility.

When you run out of options, you lose. The trick is to keep looking for alternatives and trying them until you find one that works. The next time you think, *I have no choice,* change your mind. Tell yourself, *I have many choices!* Then explore what those choices might be.

You may be surprised to find that there are always choices, if you're flexible enough to look for them. You just have to keep your mind open to the possibility of success. The moment you close your mind, the moment you stop looking for alternatives, you abandon all the other options that may be available to you, all the other chances you may have for success.

Sometimes, you have to create options when you're certain that none exist. Believe it or not, that's easy. If you can't think of anything that *will* work, make a list of everything that *won't* work. Then for each item on your list ask yourself: *But what if it could?*

When you can't think of anything you *can* do, make a list of everything you *can't* do. Then for each item on your list ask yourself: *But what if I could?*

Finally, make a list of all the options you might consider if only they weren't against the rules. Then think about how you can change the rules.

Rules—what rules?

Whenever you tell yourself *I should* or *I shouldn't*, *I must* or *I can't*, you are reciting rules. These rules may be explicit, like company policies, or they may be implicit, like the social standards of a community. Either way, they have the same effect—they limit your thinking. They allow you to consider only what is permitted instead of what is possible.

The point isn't to race out and violate every rule you can find; rules, laws, and moral codes are the threads from which every society weaves its own survival. But sometimes you have to allow yourself to think beyond the confines of the mental box in which you've been placed by your upbringing and by your culture. You need to think for yourself, instead of letting the folks who make the rules think for you. You need to consider which rules serve you and your community and which rules serve only to get in your way.

In a scene from one of the Star Trek movies, Captain Kirk was asked how he had performed in the *Kobayashi Maru* scenario, back when he was a cadet at the Star Fleet Academy. The *Kobayashi Maru* was a simulated battle in which a cadet was placed in command of a starship, surrounded by enemy vessels, and given no chance either to defeat his opponents or to escape. It was meant to be a test of character, designed to show how a cadet would perform in a no-win scenario.

The *Kobayashi Maru* problem had never been solved by a cadet—until Kirk came along. He refused to accept the no-win scenario, so he reprogrammed the battle computer to give him a chance to win. Instead of playing by the rules, he created new rules. Given no choice but to lose, he created a choice to win.

Kirk wasn't successful because he broke the rules; he was successful because he didn't let the rules break him. He opened his mind to consider what might lay beyond the rules—beyond "acceptable" behavior—and discovered an option that had eluded everyone else. To go where no cadet had gone before, he first had to think what no cadet had thought before. You have to be open to possibilities before you can recognize them as options.

Making your wish come true is a matter of how many options you give yourself to succeed. If you believe there's always one more option, one more choice, one more idea you haven't tried, then you'll always have at least one more chance for success. That's what flexibility is all about.

If what you're doing isn't working, try something else. Keep trying something else until you get what you want. You can't fail unless you run out of options. You can't run out of options unless you give up.

14

The Right Map

Imagine for a moment that you're trying to find your way around Chicago with a map of New York City. Nothing is where you expect it to be. No matter how hard you look or how far you drive, you can't get where you're trying to go. Frustrated and confused, you call your father to ask for advice. He tells you that you aren't applying yourself so you'd better get down to work. You thank him, head back into the streets, and redouble your efforts. You drive twice as hard and twice as fast, and you get lost twice as quickly.

Desperate, you call a self-help guru. You explain that you can't find a single landmark to guide you. Nothing is where it should be. You're lost, and you don't know what to do.

He says you have a bad attitude. If only you would think positively, everything would turn out all right. You hang up, race to a bookstore, and buy the latest best seller about positive thinking. You read it and get yourself so pumped up you can't see straight. With fanatical determination, you pull out your trusty map of New York, head back into the streets of Chicago, and search until you drop.

Your LAMP Plan is nothing more than a road map for success. It will work great as long as it's the right map. But if you have the wrong map, no matter how hard you try, you'll never get where you want to go.

The next time you find yourself frustrated, exhausted, working your hands to the bone with nothing to show for it, don't try to fix your attitude or your work ethic; fix your map. Here are some questions that will help:

1.   *Is your wish presentable?*

Are you going after what you want or what you don't want? Are you specific enough? Are you wishing for something you can control? You know the drill by now; go back through the steps listed in Chapter 3 and make certain your wish is presentable.

2.   *Is this wish really the most important thing for you to focus on right now?*

Maybe your priorities have changed.

3.   *Is this wish really worth the price?*

Maybe the price is higher than you thought, or maybe the payoff isn't as great as you once imagined.

4.   *How will you know when your wish has been granted?*

Maybe you already have what you want but you just haven't noticed.

5. *Are you meeting your milestones?*

    Maybe your milestones are unrealistic, or maybe they're the wrong milestones.

6. *Can your plan take you where you want to go?*

    When all the steps in your plan are completed, will they make your wish come true? Have you given yourself enough time? Have you given yourself enough money? Have you given yourself enough of all the other resources you're going to need? Is every step one that you can achieve? If your logic doesn't work or your numbers don't add up, give yourself a break: revise your plan.

7. *What do you need to do differently?*

    If what you're doing isn't working, and you keep doing it, you're going to keep getting the same results. If you want different results, try something else.

When you take the time to fix your map, you give yourself a chance to make any adjustments that might be necessary to keep you on track. You reaffirm your commitment to your wish. You allow yourself to catch your breath and return to your wish refreshed and renewed. You refocus your efforts so that all your resources can be brought to bear on whatever is holding you back. Most importantly, you give yourself the kind of motivation that can come only from certainty—the certainty that the things you're doing are the things that will work.

LAMP Process

Step Four:

Persist

15

Persistence

How many times will a baby try to take its first step before it gives up?

Babies don't know the difference between success and failure. They don't understand self-discipline. They don't know anything about courage. All they know is what they want, and they keep going until they get it.

The secret to getting what you want boils down to a single word: *persistence*. No matter how presentable your wish, how good your plan, how tireless your work, your success will ultimately hinge on persistence. Are you willing to go the distance? Then you will succeed. Are you willing to endure when others are ready to quit? Then you will succeed. Are you willing to pursue what you want until you get it, however long it takes? Then you will succeed. Success belongs to those who are unwilling to settle for less. Persist until you get what you want, and you will always get what you want.

I'm not talking about the grit-your-teeth macho kind of persistence that you read about in most self-help books.

Let other people brace themselves like mighty oaks; oaks are snapped like matchsticks before a strong wind.

The persistence I'm suggesting is the kind that outlasts whatever tries to challenge it. Armed with such persistence, you bend like a reed before the wind. When the wind passes, you remain. Your purpose remains. And your wish prevails.

Next to persistence, your skills, intelligence, and talents amount to little. The most skillful person who gives up will always finish behind the most inept person who does not. The most intelligent person who gives up will always finish behind the most simple-minded person who does not. The most talented person who gives up will always finish behind the least talented person who does not. The most gifted person alive who gives up will always finish behind someone—behind anyone—who does not.

Belief

The most common reason we give up is that we no longer believe in what we're doing. Either we don't believe our effort can succeed or we don't believe that success is worth our effort. Either way, once we lose our belief, we lose our will to continue.

And who can blame us? Why should we plant a garden unless we believe it will bear fruit? Why should we build a house unless we believe it will provide shelter? Why should we undertake personal sacrifice unless we believe that our efforts have a chance of succeeding? Why should we even get out of bed in the morning unless we believe that something worthwhile will come from the day? Without belief, there will be no effort. Without effort, there will be no results.

Belief is the foundation of persistence. Without belief,

you have no reason to complete a task. But with belief, you have no reason to quit.

Whenever you find yourself tempted to give up on a wish, ask yourself these questions:

1. *Do I believe I can make this wish come true?*
2. *Do I believe this wish is worth the effort?*

If your answer to either question is *No*, then you need to work on your belief before you work on your wish. Or you need to get a new wish.

Belief causes persistence. Persistence causes success.

16

Wish Killers

By now you have the whole world going for you. You've locked onto your wish; you're taking the appropriate action; you're managing your progress; and you're ready to persist in your efforts until you make your wish come true.

But there may yet be forces at work inside you that can make it impossible for you to succeed. I call them *wish killers* because, unchecked, that is exactly what they do.

1. *Fear*

Fear is a negative wish. The more you focus on what you fear, the more likely you are to make it happen.

Your mind does not distinguish between a mental picture of something you want and a mental picture of something you're trying to avoid. The more clearly you picture what you want, the harder your mind will work to give it to you. The more clearly you picture what you're trying to avoid, the harder your mind will work to give you that instead. Whatever you consistently picture on the inside, your mind will do its best to reproduce on the outside. Unless you want to make your fears come true, think of something else.

I learned how to do that when I was a little boy. Like most youngsters, I was afraid of getting a shot, so I had to find some way to control my panic whenever my Mom led me into the doctor's office. I learned to think about things I really enjoyed—like Disneyland, and birthday presents, and hot fudge sundaes—anything to get my mind off what was about to happen. It was a silly little trick, but it worked. It still works, for all kinds of fears. And now I know why.

When you're afraid, the movie you're running in your mind is likely to be a gut-wrenching feature presentation of what you fear. You react to that movie the same way you react to a good horror movie—with sweaty palms, a churning stomach, a racing heart. Change the movie, and you change your reaction.

I'm not telling you to deny your fear or to sweep it under the carpet. I'm not suggesting that you try to minimize the danger or the discomfort of whatever it is you're afraid of. I'm simply suggesting that you think about something else. Throw another film in the projector and watch what happens.

For example, what would you do if you found yourself watching an unpleasant show on TV? You would change the channel, right? You can do exactly the same thing when you find yourself watching an unpleasant show in your mind: you can change the channel and watch something else.

When you're afraid of something, you're picturing what can go wrong. If you want to change the channel, picture what can go right, instead. Instead of picturing the worst thing that can happen, picture the best thing that can happen. Instead of picturing the pain, picture the gain. Instead of picturing what you have to lose, picture what you have to win.

When you change the movie you're watching in your mind, you change your emotional reaction to it. You turn your fear into excitement, your dread into anticipation, your avoidance into action. You can accomplish all of this simply by changing your mental pictures.

Is it really that easy? Yes and no. The movies you're running in your mind are a matter of habit. Changing one of these movies is as difficult, or as easy, as changing any other habit.

You already know how to change your habits. You know how to use visualization, affirmation, pre-memory, and the Thirty Day Plan. So go ahead and use these tools to teach yourself a new habit, the habit of running a new movie, a movie in which you picture what you have to win instead of what you have to lose. With this new habit, your fear will lose its power over you forever.

2.   *Thinking like a victim*

The second wish killer is to think like a victim. As Webster defines it, a victim is "someone harmed by or suffering from some act, condition, or circumstance."

Do you know anyone who doesn't fit that description? We're all victimized by something—crime, discrimination, poverty, a handicap, a broken home, a lousy boss, flyaway hair. But the only real victim is the person who thinks like one.

Life is a self-service gas station. You can sit in your car and honk, or you can fill the tank yourself. No one honks longer, louder, or with less effect than a victim.

It's easy to think like a victim. For one thing, it feels good. It lets you off the hook. When you're not responsible for what happens to you, you can't be expected to do anything about it. When the cards are stacked against you, you have no choice but to fold, so you never have to face the pressure of playing to win. And you never lack for something to do. You can fill every idle moment with the bittersweet memories of your misfortunes. Unfortunately, you can never fulfill your wishes.

When you think like a victim, you turn yourself from a cause into an effect. Nothing can kill a wish faster than that. When you blame the world, you lose your power to change it. In the name of what you can't fix, you sacrifice what you can.

It's not what happens to you that counts, it's what you choose to do about it. We are all victims of forces beyond our control. The people who get what they want from life are the ones who focus on forces they can control. They choose to live as a cause instead of as an effect.

If you want to become a cause in your own life, don't think like an effect. Instead of worrying about the cards you've been dealt, play them. Instead of asking, *Why me?* ask, *What am I going to do about it?* Instead of feeling sorry for yourself, refuse to settle for less than what you want.

The world owes you only what you're willing to collect. The way to collect is to make your wishes come true.

17

The Myth
of Self-Discipline

Success flows from passion, not from self-discipline. I'm not suggesting that self-discipline is unimportant. Just the opposite. Self-discipline is the foundation of character; character is the foundation of all lasting success. The headlines and the history books are full of hotshots who fell from grace because they lacked character. Without character, success is meaningless.

But character is only the launching pad, it's not the rocket. The rocket is passion.

Successful people do what they need to do whether they like it or not. That's self-discipline. *Exceptionally* successful people do what they need to do because they love it. That's passion.

If you have to force yourself to make your wish come true, you're working on the wrong wish. Look around you. The people who are wildly successful aren't doing what they hate; they're doing what they love. Or at least they've learned to love what they're doing.

It's easy to fall in love with an effect—we all want to be rich, or famous, or to make a difference in the world—the trick is to fall in love with the cause. The people most likely to become successful, however you measure success, are the ones who fall in love with the processes that cause their success. Fall in love with the cause, and the effect will take care of itself.

When you're in love with the cause, you're following the path of least resistance. Your actions come naturally. You don't have to discipline yourself, you don't have to force yourself, you don't even have to motivate yourself. You simply do what you enjoy doing. The 'doing' then becomes its own reward, and your desired results follow the way dessert follows a great meal.

When you're passionately in love with the process of making your wish come true, you allow yourself to treasure the moment, instead of waiting for some distant payoff. This is what living is all about. The greatest gift you can give yourself is to enjoy today. Why do you think they call it "the present"?

The easiest way to substitute passion for self-discipline is to change the way you think about what you're doing. Instead of asking yourself *How can I get myself to do this?* ask yourself *How can I get myself to enjoy doing this?* The secret to joy is to find it wherever you look, and to look for it everywhere. Look for it in the tasks that will make your wish come true. Look for it in the 'doing'. Look for it in the challenges you face and the problems you have to solve. Look for it in the moment.

Don't try to talk yourself into feeling this joy, imagine yourself into it instead. Change your mental movie. Enlarge your comfort zone. Instead of running a movie that shows how much you hate what you're doing, run a movie that shows how much you love it. Picture how much you enjoy doing the things that will make your wish come true, and before long you'll enjoy doing them.

At first this new movie might feel uncomfortable, the way you feel when you're trying to acquire any new habit. Just keep practicing until it feels more natural to run the new movie than it does to run the old one.

When you run your new movie, allow yourself to feel the intense emotions you have already connected with your wish. Whatever you deeply feel for your wish, you will soon feel for each step that causes your wish to come true. When you allow yourself to connect positive emotions to every step you take along the way, you soon find yourself performing every step naturally, without self-discipline. No matter what step you're working on, you feel the emotional satisfaction of working on your entire wish. When you reach that point, causing your wish to come true will seem like the most natural thing in the world, a product of passion and joy, instead of harsh discipline.

18

Play The Pauses

To make music you have to play the pauses, not just the notes. To make a wish, you have to do the same. You have to give yourself moments to relax, to do nothing, to take a breath before moving to the next task.

To persist you must first endure. To endure, you must from time to time allow yourself to recuperate. Nature shows us the way. Summer's frantic growth is offset by the slumber of Winter. The violence of a storm relaxes in its aftermath. Creatures great and small labor during the day, and lie up at night. In all that it does, Nature builds a balance between exertion and relaxation. We are smart to build that same balance into our own lives.

Even machines take a break. In the life cycle of a machine there is a balance between operation and maintenance. If you don't maintain the machine—change the oil, recharge the battery, lubricate the moving parts—it will burn itself out. The same is true for people.

People who are successful over the long haul don't allow themselves to burn out. They know how to recuperate.

They know how to relax. They know how to play the pauses, along with the notes. They have the discipline to know when to quit.

That's right, quit. When the going gets tough, the tough quit. They take a break. They distance themselves from the situation so they can gain a fresh perspective. They recharge their batteries so they can come back stronger and more effective than ever. You don't read much about this in self-help books. The biographies of great achievers don't dwell on recovery. But at the heart of success, at the core of all achievement, you're always going to find pauses, not just notes.

There is no better example than Winston Churchill. He was a juggernaut—supercharged with energy, ceaselessly active, unstoppable, perhaps the greatest achiever of the Twentieth Century. How did he do it? He took a nap every day. Even in the darkest months of World War II, when bombs fell nightly on London and hope seemed lost for Britain and perhaps for all of Western Civilization, Churchill took his naps. He kept himself going when others would have collapsed. He kept himself going by knowing when to stop.

If you feel stressed, or depressed, or worn out, if you feel ready to give up, the chances are you don't know when to stop. To make your wishes come true, you need to pace yourself, not kill yourself. You need to play the pauses.

How you pause is your business. It may be by parachute jumping or rock climbing. It may be by lying in your hammock all afternoon, or baking a pie. It may be by watching a movie, or reading a book, or painting a picture. Whatever works for you, do it. Do it often. Build it into your LAMP Plan. Notes without pauses aren't music, they're just noise.

19

Follow-Through

Plan Your Finish

I once attended a seminar where one of the exercises called for us to climb a 50-foot telephone pole, stand on the top, and leap to a trapeze. The object was to learn how to overcome our fears, presumably without killing ourselves in the process (there was a harness to break the fall). Being terrified of heights, I couldn't resist.

To psyche myself up to face the challenge, I pictured the process from start to finish as clearly and precisely as if it were already a memory. I ascended the pole; I balanced at the top; I leaped to the trapeze; I practiced the whole thing over and over in my mind before I tried it with my body.

Then I did it, just the way I pictured it. I climbed the pole; I stood on top; I kept my balance in the stiff breeze. And I jumped flawlessly. I sailed through the air and reached for the bar like I was an Olympic gymnast. Then a curious thing happened. As my body swung out into space

50 feet above the ground, the force of the jump tore my hands from the bar. And I fell.

The harness caught me, just the way it was supposed to. As the spotters lowered me gently to the ground, all I could think about was how badly I blew it. *What went wrong?*

Nothing went wrong. I accomplished exactly what I set out to accomplish. But I hadn't set out to accomplish enough. I hadn't planned my finish.

It never occurred to me that I might need to make a special effort to hold on to the trapeze. I planned the climb. I planned how to keep my balance on the pole. I planned the jump. I planned how I would reach out with perfect form and grab the bar. I just never planned to hold on. I didn't follow through in my mind, so I didn't follow through with my body.

In your LAMP Plan, make sure you've included every step necessary to take you where you want to go—including the last one, the one that completes your follow-through and gets you there. Plan your finish, or your plan is finished.

Finish Your Plan

Sometimes when you're nearing the end of a long and demanding wish, you feel an almost irresistible urge to let down, to relax. Resist it. It's like that warm, cozy feeling you get just before you fall asleep in the snow and freeze to death.

I know I told you to play the pauses, but not when you're beginning the last lap of a race, not when you've almost pushed the boulder to the top of the hill, not when you're about to make your wish come true. If you relax before the finish, you may never finish. Or you may finish second when you've set your heart on finishing first.

If you feel like relaxing, relax after you've finished and not a moment before. What good is a whodunit one page short of who did it? What good is a boat one plank shy of a bottom? What good is the fastest runner if he never finishes a race, or the ablest politician if he never completes a campaign? What good is the finest surgeon in the world if he never sews you back together?

You get the picture. Finish what you start.

Know What Comes Next

What if the harder you worked, the more likely you were to find yourself out of a job? That's the position you put your subconscious in when you near the end of one wish without having another one in the queue.

When you created your LAMP Plan, you penciled in your next wish. Part of your follow-through is to begin to focus attention on that wish. Not enough to divert you from your current wish, but enough to let your subconscious mind know there's plenty more work where that came from.

Not that you shouldn't take a break between wishes. Take a week off; take a month off; take a year off. Reward yourself with a vacation. Do whatever you need to do to recharge your power cells. Meanwhile, in the back of your mind, know what comes next.

20

Wake Up

Other animals spend their lives locked in a cycle of instinct. When they're hungry, they eat. When they hear a loud noise, they run. When they're attacked, they fight. When they come into season, they mate. They live the way their genes and their environment have programmed them to live because they have no choice. But we do.

We, too, are programmed by our genes and by our environment. But we can transcend our programming. We have been given the awesome power not just to respond to what the world throws at us, but to *choose* our response. We can program ourselves.

Alone among the animals, we have what it takes to make our lives serve our own ends instead of the ends that have been handed down to us. We can break the chain of events that has shaped us and learn to shape ourselves. We have been given the Godlike power to participate in our own fate. But not one in ten of us knows it.

Like the elephant, we are unconscious of our own strength. When it comes to understanding the power we have to make a difference in our own lives, we might as well be asleep.

If you want to make your wishes come true, *wake up*. Wake up to your own strength. Wake up to the role you play in your own destiny. Wake up to the power you have to choose what you think, do, and say.

The moment you understand that your life is whatever you make of it by choice, you will awaken to an astonishing new world. Like an elephant who suddenly realizes he's the strongest animal in the jungle, you will become aware of the limitless possibilities that surround you. You will feel at once a sense of humility and power; humility because all of life is a gift; power because you've been given the most potent gift of all—*the power to choose*. But you can exercise this power only when you're awake.

To wake up is to grow up. As children, we are by nature dependent. As adults, all too often we maintain that dependence. We rely on others, or on circumstances, to give us what we want, instead of taking that responsibility upon ourselves. But once we wake up to the power of choice, once we become aware our own strength, we become forever independent. Once we realize that we can give ourselves what we want, we're no longer content to rely on others.

Nor are we willing to accept only what the world feels like giving us. The moment we realize all that we can give ourselves, we refuse to settle for less.

Waking up is like coming to your senses. You see things more clearly than ever before. You feel a greater sense of freedom, a greater sense of possibility. Your limitations are limitations no more. You see them for what they really are— bad dreams. And then they quickly lose their power over you the way a nightmare loses it edge the moment you awaken. You find yourself free to imagine more useful thoughts, to dream more pleasant dreams, and to turn those dreams into reality.

The difference between being asleep and being awake is the difference between having a dream and making that dream come true. That's what happens when you're awake. That's the kind of gift you can give yourself when you know your own strength.

Conclusion

Remember the Class of '53 from Yale University? Only 3% of them had written goals. The others knew the power of setting goals, but they elected not to make use of that power.

The world is full of people like that. Ask a group of men and women how many of them understand the value of setting goals, and every one will raise a hand. But ask how many of them actually set goals, and you'll be likely to see the same 3% response.

Almost everyone knows the power of goal-setting, and almost everyone ignores it. It's tempting to ask why, but that's the wrong question. The right question is this: *What are* you *going to do about it?*

Are you going to make your wishes come true, or are you going to keep on doing what you've been doing? Are you going to turn the LAMP Process into a habit, or are you going to settle back into your comfort zone and let the next ten years pass the way the last ten did? They will, unless you cause something different to happen.

This book is not about success. It's not about happiness. It's not about personal fulfillment. It's about cause and effect. It shows you step by step how to set in motion the appropriate causes that will produce whatever effects you want. But a book can do no more than lead you to water. You have to decide if you're thirsty enough to take a drink.

With all my heart I would love to be able to flip a little switch in your mind that would activate your magic lamp and supercharge you with enough energy and self-awareness to make your wishes come true for the rest of your life. But I can't do that. Only you can flip that switch. Only you can make that one choice that makes everything else possible. The best I can do is to leave you with this thought:

Wishing works, if you do.

Lend a Copy to a Friend

There is nothing more useless than a book sitting on a bookshelf; there is nothing more powerful than the same book in the hands of someone who can use it. If you think *The Magic Lamp* is worth reading, please lend your copy to a friend. Pass it around. Wear it out. Let others benefit from your investment the way you have.

If you prefer to keep your own copy, you can order gift copies by completing the order form at the back of this book or by contacting Three Waters Press at the address listed below.

Success Stories

Would you like to have your success story published in the next edition of *The Magic Lamp*? Just send us a letter or an Email message describing your wish and telling us how *The Magic Lamp* helped you make it come true. If your story is one of those selected for publication, we'll send you a copy of the revised edition autographed by the author and complete with a new chapter full of success stories—including your own.

Send your success story to:

THREE WATERS PRESS
349 Turkey Ridge Road
Suite 100
Boston, Virginia 22713
Phone: 540-547-3537
Fax: 540-547-4245
Internet: lamp@selfhelp.com

Resources

In writing *The Magic Lamp*, I've borrowed freely from dozens of books and tapes I've come across during the past two decades. The short directory that follows is a list of the best of these resources, organized by category, so you can pinpoint the works most likely to help you acquire or master the skills you need to make your wishes come true.

Achievement

Awake the Giant Within, Anthony Robbins; Summit Books, New York, NY

> One of the great books about developing your potential. Robbins blends his version of NLP (neurolinguistic programming) with unique insights into personal development. *Giant* provides one of the most complete and detailed guides available for making changes in your life.

The Neuropsychology of Achievement (cassette album); Sybervision, Pleasanton, CA

> A useful set of cassettes about how you can "wire"

your brain for achievement. The material is excellent; the delivery is by a professional narrator, so it lacks the passion of the person who actually developed the ideas.

The Path of Least Resistance, Robert Fritz; Stillpoint Publishing, Salem, MA

Fritz provides useful insight into the power and process of making choices.

Wishcraft, Barbara Sher, with Annie Gottlieb; Ballantine, New York, NY

A highly readable and down to earth look at how to get what you want from life. Sher (and Gottlieb) offer particularly useful information about how to make plans, how to schedule those plans, and how to get other people to help you make your dreams come true.

Creativity

Creative Thinking (cassette album), Mike Vance; Nightingale-Conant, Niles, IL

If you think creativity is something you're either born with or you're not, you're half right—everyone is born with it. But most of us don't know how to put it to use. This cassette album shows you the way.

The Creative Mystique, How to Manage It, Nurture It, and Make It Pay (cassette), John M. Keil; Wiley Sound Business, New York, NY

A brief and informative program about how you can tap your creativity to improve your life.

Happiness

Chicken Soup For The Soul: 101 Stories To Open The Heart And Rekindle The Spirit, written and compiled by Jack Canfield and Mark Victor Hansen; Health Communications, Inc, Deerfield Beach, FL

If you like inspirational stories, you'll treasure this book; it's a delightful collection of them.

First Things First, Stephen R. Covey, A. Roger Merrill, Rebecca R. Merrill ; Simon & Schuster, New York, NY

This book is a "Must Read" because it get to the heart of finding happiness and fulfillment amidst the stresses and strains of living in the Nineties. If you want to find out how to set your life on it's proper course and keep it there, read this book.

Flow, The Psychology of Optimal Experience, Mihaly Csikszentmihaly; Harper Perennial, New York

Another "Must Read". If you've ever had one of those moments when you felt on top of the world, you'll love *Flow* because it explains how you got there and how you can get back.

This isn't just a good book, it's an important book. It does a remarkably good job of performing an almost impossible task: explaining the mystery of happiness and showing you how to achieve it.

Man's Search For Meaning, An Introduction To Logotherapy, Victor E. Frankl; Touchstone, New York

"Meaning" is the most common denominator among the various philosophies of happiness. Where people find meaning, they usually find happiness.

In this moving and profound book, Dr. Frankl shows how human beings can find meaning where they least expect it, even under the most oppressive of circumstances. As the backdrop for this theme, he relates his own experiences as an inmate in the Nazi death camps during World War II.

The Evolving Self, A Psychology For The Third Millennium, Mihaly Csikszentmihaly; Harper Perennial, New York

This wonderful book reviews and refines the insights contained in *Flow* (see above) and develops them into a powerful model for how to live a life that maximizes joy, fulfillment, and happiness.

The Road Less Traveled, M. Scott Peck, MD; Touchstone, New York, NY

A "Must Read". This is one of those rare books that makes you a better person simply from having read it. You learn about psychology, about yourself, and about how to live the kind of life that both rewards and fulfills you—and leaves the world a better place.

Getting Published

How to Get Happily Published, 4th Edition, Judith

Appelbaum; Harper Perennial, New York, NY

If you think getting a book published is a mystery, here's the book that will demystify the process for you. Not only does it show you how to go about finding an agent and a publisher, but also how to promote the book when it's published.

How to Publish a Book & Sell a Million Copies, Ted Nicholas; Enterprise•Dearborn Publishing

If you've already decided to publish a book yourself (or if you're considering it) this book will show you how to go about it and how to market it after you publish it.

Insider's Guide to Book Editors, Publishers, and Literary Agents, 1994-1995, Jeff Herman; Prima Publishing, Rocklin, CA

This is the only source I know that identifies key people in publishing firms and agencies, along with their special areas of interest, so that you can contact the people who are most likely to be interested in what you've written.

The Self-Publishing Manual, How to Write, Print and Sell Your Own Book, Dan Poynter; Para Publishing, Santa Barbara, CA

If you would like to see your name on the cover of a book, read this one. It contains more good and useful information about self-publishing than any other single source I've read.

Leadership

Principle Centered Leadership (cassette program), Stephen R. Covey; Nightingale-Conant, Niles, IL

An excellent program that applies Covey's ideas about principle-centered living to help solve the problems of leadership.

The One Minute Manager, Kenneth Blanchard, Ph.D., Spencer Johnson, MD.; William Morrow and Company, New York, NY

A phenomenal success when it came out more than a decade ago, this little book is still setting sales records, and with good reason. If you want to learn some of the most important principles for successfully managing people, this is a great place to start.

Learning

Writing To Learn, William Zinsser; HarperCollins, New York, NY

If you really want to learn something, write about it. Zinsser shows you how.

Memory

The Memory Book, Harry Lorayne and Jerry Lucas; Ballantine Books, New York, NY

Everyone is born with a terrific memory, but only

the lucky few ever learn how to use it. This book shows how you can become one of them. If you would like to develop your ability to remember names, facts, and other information, this book will help you do it.

Mega Memory (cassette album), Kevin Trudeau; The American Memory Institute, New York, NY

This cassette album will help you remember anything you want, from names to faces to facts. If you would like to have a better memory—but think you weren't "born with it"—think again, and listen to these tapes.

Negotiating

Getting To Yes, Roger Fisher and William Ury; Penguin Books, New York, NY

To turn opponents into supporters, you have to learn to negotiate what the experts call a "win-win" agreement. This short book is one of the most straightforward and widely read guides for doing just that.

Power Negotiating, (cassette program), Roger Dawson; Nightingale-Conant, Niles, IL

This audio program is full of hard-ball tricks and techniques for negotiating toward a win-win agreement.

Win-Win Negotiating, Turning Conflict Into Agreement (cassette), Fred E. Jandt, with Paul Gillette; Wiley Sound Business, New York, NY

This is a shorter (and cheaper) cassette program, that provides a good introduction to the principles of effective negotiation.

Neurolinguistic Programming

The Structure of Magic, Vols. I & II, Richard Bandler and John Grinder; Science and Behavior Books, Inc., Palo Alto, CA

The men who gave us Neurolinguistic Programming (NLP), Richard Bandler and John Grinder, set out originally to create a method by which anyone could master any skill—what you might call a science of human achievement. Their efforts produced one of the most elegant and powerful models of human communication.

This model shed new and welcome light on how we communicate with ourselves (to learn new behavior, for example), and how we communicate with others. During the past two decades, NLP has influenced many disciplines, including education, psychotherapy, sports, business, and sales.

These two volumes are the first that Bandler and Grinder published about their research. They're dry and difficult reading, and they're brilliant. If you want to understand where NLP came from, read them. If you simply want to understand how NLP can be of use to you, read *Unlimited Power* (below).

Unlimited Power, Anthony Robbins; Simon and Schuster, New York, NY

A "Must Read". This is the book that brought NLP

to a mass audience. As a blueprint for achievement and success, it remains unequaled. Robbins combines some of the most powerful techniques from NLP with his own useful and profound insights into human nature. He provides a readable, entertaining, and invaluable guide to making the most of your life.

Persuasion

How To Win Friends and Influence People, Dale Carnegie; Pocket Books, New York, NY

If you don't count ancient scripture, this is the best book there is about how to get along with other people.

Influence, The New Psychology of Persuasion, Robert B. Cialdini; Ph.D., Quill, New York, NY

You would be amazed at how often each day you are influenced in ways that you would never dream about. You would also be amazed at how easy it is to become a more powerful influencer yourself. If you would like to master the skills of persuasion and influence, this book is a superb tool to help you do it.

Problem Solving

The Art and Science of Problem Solving (cassette album), Bill Gibson; Nightingale-Conant, Niles, IL

Don't wish for fewer problems, wish for more skills to solve them. This cassette album is a good place to start. It gives you a wealth of techniques and exercises for how to develop your innate problem solving ability.

Self-Image

How To Have High Self-Esteem (cassette album), Jack Canfield; Nightingale-Conant, Niles, IL

Having low self-esteem is like swimming upstream backwards. There are very few problems on this planet that aren't in some way connected to low self-esteem, either your own, or someone else's. You can't do much about someone else's self-esteem, but you can do yours a world of good. Canfield will show you how.

Succeeding Through Inner Strength (cassette album), Nathaniel Branden; Nightingale-Conant, Niles, IL

If you find yourself wishing for the strength to face a great challenge, you'll find these tapes a wonderful catalyst for building that strength. Full of wisdom, humanity, and practical advice, Branden's program helps you develop self esteem at the same time that you're developing intestinal fortitude.

Selling

SPIN Selling, Neil Rackham; McGraw-Hill, New York, NY

If you're in sales and you're looking for a competitive edge, read this book.

Major Account Sales Strategy, Neil Rackham; McGraw-Hill, New York, NY

If you sell to major accounts and you're looking for a competitive edge, read this book.

Strategic Selling, Robert B. Miller, Steven E. Heiman, with Tad Tuleja; Warner Books, New York, NY

If you're in the business of making complex sales (i.e., in your accounts you have to persuade more than one person to buy before you make a sale), and you want to make yourself as close to unbeatable as a salesperson can get, read all three of these books (*SPIN Selling, Major Account Sales Strategy, and Strategic Selling*).

Self-Discipline

Neuropsychology of Self-Discipline (cassette album); Sybervision

This album shows you how to use the advanced learning techniques, developed by Neuroscientist Karl Pribram, in order to master self-discipline. The content is superb; the narration is done by a professional, rather than by Dr. Pribram himself, so you lose something in the translation.

Sleep

The Sleep Management Plan, Dale Hanson Bourke; Harper Paperbacks, New York, NY

If you would like to spend less time sleeping and more time doing what you wish, this book can show you how. (But consult your physician before you start messing around with your sleeping habits.)

Speaking

Change Your Voice, Change Your Life, Dr. Morton Cooper; Harper & Row, New York

> Your voice has a great deal to do with how other people respond to you. This book shows how you've chosen the voice you have, and how you can choose to modify that voice to make yourself a more effective communicator.

How To Get Your Point Across in 30 Seconds—Or Less, Milo O. Frank; Simon and Schuster, New York, NY

> If you can't make your point in under 30 seconds, you don't understand what you're trying to say. Frank shows you how to distill even a complex idea into something you can communicate in less time than it takes the average person to tune you out.

Public Speaking (cassette album), Earl Nightingale; Nightingale-Conant, Niles, IL

> This cassette program shares with you the insights that helped make Earl Nightingale one of the most admired and requested speakers in the country.

Put Your Money Where Your Mouth Is, How To Make A Fortune In Public Speaking, Robert Anthony, Ph.D.; Berkley Books, New York, NY

If you've ever fantasized about earning a living as an "expert", jetting around the country, staying in fancy hotels, and being paid a lot of money to talk about things that interest you, it doesn't have to be a fantasy. Dr. Anthony's book shows you how to make that kind of dream come true.

Success

Do What You Love And The Money Will Follow, Marsha Sinetar; Dell, New York, NY

Sinetar makes the simple but profound argument that if you figure out what you really want to do with your life, and then do it, you'll make all the money you need. And then she shows you how.

Personal Power, A 30 Day Program for Unlimited Success (cassette series), Anthony Robbins; Guthy-Renker Corporation, Irwindale, CA

These tapes form one of the most powerful programs for personal change ever recorded. They provide a 30 day strategy that helps you firmly set your course on achieving what you've always dreamed about.

The Art of Exceptional Living (cassette album), Jim Rohn; Nightingale-Conant, Niles, IL

Ever wonder where inspirational writers get their inspiration? From people like Jim Rohn. This cassette album is pithy, useful, and crammed with advice that really can make a difference in your life.

The Essence of Success (cassette library), Earl Nightingale; Nightingale-Conant, Niles, IL

Earl Nightingale's album, *The Strangest Secret*, recorded in the 1950s, was the first self-help album to sell a million copies. He devoted his life to studying success and achievement and then sharing with others what he had learned. What set him apart was that he took the time to master the arts of communication—he was a compelling writer, public speaker, and broadcaster—so that he could better convey the information he had made it his mission to share.

The Essence of Success is really "The Essence of Earl Nightingale". It's a delightful and thought provoking distillation of thousands of hours of his daily radio programs, cassette albums, and interviews, worth every moment you invest in listening to it, and every penny you invest in buying a copy for your own library.

The New Lead The Field (cassette album), Earl Nightingale; Nightingale-Conant, Niles, IL

Nightingale recorded dozens of albums and cassette programs, many of them culled from the daily radio broadcasts he made during a career that spanned decades. *The New Lead The Field* was an update of an earlier bestselling album (*Lead The Field*). It was one of his last full-length programs, and one of his best, filled with wisdom and practical advice about how to make your life everything you've ever wanted it to be.

The Seven Spiritual Laws of Success, Deepak Chopra; Co-published by Amber-Allen Publishing and New World Library, San Rafael, CA

Deepak Chopra is both a medical doctor, trained in the latest technologies of modern healing, and a practitioner of Ayurvedic medicine, a body of knowledge handed down from ancient India. With his unique grasp of what is useful from the East and from the West, from the new and from the old, he dispenses the most profound insights as matter of factly as the rest of us might talk about the latest sports scores, or our favorite TV shows. This little book (116 pages) is a wise and gentle introduction to the spiritual principles that underlie a successful life.

The Seven Habits of Highly Successful People, Stephen R. Covey; Simon and Schuster, New York, NY

Covey has a way of putting his finger on the most important issues facing those who wish to live a successful and fulfilling life. *The Seven Habits* shows you how to reap the rewards of a life based on principle, character, and a commitment to conscience.

The Strangest Secret (cassette album), Earl Nightingale; Nightingale-Conant, Niles, IL

Thirty years after he released the original recording of *The Strangest Secret*, the album that launched an entire industry, Earl Nightingale recorded a full-length cassette album with the same title. In it he reviews his original thinking about success, and enhances it with insights drawn from an additional three decades of study, experience, and reflection.

Think And Grow Rich, by Napoleon Hill; Fawcett, New York, NY

This is the book that spawned the self-help movement. It wasn't the first self-help book, to be sure, but it was the one that caught fire, and it's the one that almost everybody else refers back to. This is the book in which Earl Nightingale first read the words that he later made famous in *The Strangest Secret* ("You are what you think about"). This is the book that for many of today's leading self-help thinkers served as their introduction to the fundamentals of success.

Thinking

The Power of Focused Thinking (cassette album), Edward de Bono; The International Center for Creative Thinking, Mamaroneck, NY

Most of us have never learned how to think. We just do what comes naturally to us, without trying to do it better, or do it right. But de Bono has devoted his career to studying the nature of thinking, and to communicating his insights to the rest of us so that we can get the most from our mental abilities.

The material in this album is excellent, even though it's performed by a professional narrator, rather than by the author himself.

Time Management

How To Get Control Of Your Time And Your Life, Alan Lakein; Signet, New York, NY

This is one of the best and most widely read books about how to make the most of your time. If you don't have the time to read this book—boy, do you need it!

Time for Success, A Goal-setter's Strategy; R. Alec Mackenzie; McGraw-Hill, New York, NY

Mackenzie, one of the most respected experts in the field, presents a solid strategy for how to put your time to the most effective use.

Writing

The Elements of Style, William Strunk, Jr. and E.B. White; MacMillan Co. New York, NY

Someone once said that every writer should read this book at least once a year. And you don't have to be a professional writer to benefit. Anyone who puts words to paper would do well to read this compact, pithy masterpiece.

On Writing Well, Fifth Edition, William Zinsser; HarperCollins, New York, NY

A "Must Read".

Like most people, I did a lot of writing when I was in school. But I never learned how to write until long after I had graduated.

The best advice I ever found on writing, I found in this book. In a couple hundred delightful pages, Zinsser shows you how to write with clarity, simplicity, and humanity—the kind of writing that people will read.

If you write at all—at work, as a hobby, for correspondence—and if you want your readers to comprehend what you're trying to say, I urge you to study this book and practice what it preaches.

The Writer's Art, James J. Kilpatrick; Andrews and McMeel, Kansas City, MO

Kilpatrick's book is a joy to read. His writing is a stroll through a garden of fresh metaphor. With examples, and by example, he shows you how to add snap, crackle, and pop to whatever you want to say.

Equally rewarding, and unique in what I've read, Kilpatrick stresses the importance of cadence to good writing. He provides examples from the writings of others, but none are as enlightening as his own rhythmic prose.

Index

H

About The Author

Keith Ellis is a *Magna Cum Laude* graduate of Georgetown University. He lives and writes in Rappahannock County, Virginia, in the foothills of the Blue Ridge Mountains.

One Spring morning a few years back, he asked himself a simple question: "What do I wish I had known about success when I was 18 years old?" His answer became *The Magic Lamp*.

He welcomes any comments you have about this book.

Speaking Engagements

Keith Ellis has been described as one of the most dynamic and inspirational speakers in the nation. If you would like him to address your organization, call or write:

Keith Ellis
c/o
THREE WATERS PRESS
349 Turkey Ridge Road
Suite 100
Boston, Virginia 22713
Phone: 540-547-3537
Fax: 540-547-4245
Internet: lamp@selfhelp.com

Order Form

Fax Orders: Fax this form to (540) 547-4245

Telephone orders: Call Toll Free: (800) 738-5267; please have your VISA or Mastercard ready.

On-line orders: send an Email message to lamp@selfhelp.com; please include your VISA or Mastercard number, the name as it appears on your card, and the expiration date.

The Magic Lamp ($14.95)   Quantity _____
The Magic Lamp T-shirt ($19.95)   Quantity _____

Company name: _____

Name: _____

Address: _____

City: _____

Telephone: (   ) _____

Sales Tax:
Please add 4.5% for books shipped to addresses in Virginia.

Shipping:
Please add $3.95 for the first item; $1.50 for each additional item.

Payment:
☐ Check
☐ Credit card: ☐ VISA   ☐ Mastercard

Card number: _____ Exp. date: _____
Name on card: _____

Call *toll free* and order now

Order Form

Fax Orders: Fax this form to (540) 547-4245

Telephone orders: Call Toll Free: (800) 738-5267; please have your VISA or Mastercard ready.

On-line orders: send an Email message to lamp@selfhelp.com; please include your VISA or Mastercard number, the name as it appears on your card, and the expiration date.

The Magic Lamp ($14.95)   Quantity _____
The Magic Lamp T-shirt ($19.95)   Quantity _____

Company name: _____

Name: _____

Address: _____

City: _____

Telephone: (   ) _____

Sales Tax:
Please add 4.5% for books shipped to addresses in Virginia.

Shipping:
Please add $3.95 for the first item; $1.50 for each additional item.

Payment:
☐ Check
☐ Credit card: ☐VISA ☐ Mastercard

Card number: _____ Exp. date: _____
Name on card: _____

Call *toll free* and order now

Order Form

Fax Orders: Fax this form to (540) 547-4245

Telephone orders: Call Toll Free: (800) 738-526'
VISA or Mastercard ready.

On-line orders: send an Email message to lamp@
include your VISA or Mastercard number, the nai
your card, and the expiration date.

The Magic Lamp ($14.95)   Quantity __
The Magic Lamp T-shirt ($19.95)   Quantity __

Company name: _____

Name: _____

Address: _____

City: _____

Telephone: (   ) _____

Sales Tax:
Please add 4.5% for books shipped to addresses in Vir

Shipping:
Please add $3.95 for the first item; $1.50 for each addit

Payment:
☐ Check
☐ Credit card: ☐ VISA ☐ Mastercard

Card number: _____ Ex
Name on card: _____

Call *toll free* and order now